THE SUCCESSFUL EXECUTIVE

Acknowledgments

Some of the people I have worked with showed me what to do and some what not to do. I remember and thank you all.

Other business authors have proved inspirational, from Napoleon Hill to Norman Vincent Peale, from Anthony Robbins' *Powertalks* to Stephen Covey's *Seven Habits*. If you can't get inspiration from this book, do get it somewhere else.

My wife, Sue, teaches me almost every day. My father – who kindly made many useful alterations – and mother still teach me, as increasingly do my children. Now there's an executive challenge. Richard Linacre provided lots of pointers and, once again, Sheila Bull made scores of suggestions and improvements for which I am, as always, grateful. Thank you team.

THE SUCCESSFUL EXECUTIVE

HOW TO SCALE THE MANAGEMENT LADDER SWIFTLY AND SURELY

Nigel Linacre

C
CENTURY
**BUSINESS
BOOKS**

First published in 1997 by Century Ltd
Random House, 20 Vauxhall Bridge Road, London SW1V 2SA

Random House Australia (Pty) Limited
20 Alfred Street, Milsons Point,
Sydney, New South Wales 2061, Australia

Random House New Zealand Limited
18 Poland Road, Glenfield
Auckland 10, New Zealand

Random House South Africa (Pty) Limited
Endulini, 5a Jubilee Road, Parktown 2193, South Africa

Random House UK Limited Reg. No. 954009

Papers used by Random House UK Limited are natural, recyclable products made from wood grown in sustainable forests. The manufacturing processes conform to the environmental regulations of the country of origin.

ISBN 0 7126 7866 2

Companies, institutions and other organizations wishing to make bulk purchases of any business books published by Random House should contact their local bookstore or Random House direct:
Special Sales Director,
Random House, 20 Vauxhall Bridge Road, London SW1V 2SA
Tel: 0171 840 8470 Fax 0171 828 6681

Typeset by Palimpsest Book Production Limited,
Polmont, Stirlingshire
Printed and bound in Great Britain by
Mackays of Chatham plc, Chatham, Kent

Contents

Chapter One

Firm Foundations

1.1 Why you should read this book

The issue is what you take out of it

Here's the deal. Read this book and you'll probably be a more successful executive. Apply what's in the book and you certainly will. Return and re-apply what you learn, and you will get more effective because the more time and effort you put into the process, the more you will get out of it.

You may have read books on goal-setting and success, on time management and personal organization, and on writing and presenting effectively, but you may not have found them all in one book. Now you have. *The Successful Executive* can help you to improve your performance in all of these areas and more. Whether you have been an executive for many years or are relatively new to business, whether you work in a big or a small firm, or for national or local government or one of their agencies, *The Successful Executive* could help you to be more successful.·

The first section is about the basic habits of business effectiveness. They are often taken for granted, but seldom learnt well. Without them, work will always be fraught with difficulty. The second is about the organizational skills and habits you need to use to be on top of your work. The third shows you how complementary time management practices can help you get on top of your schedule. The fourth is about effective communication, without which team work is impossible. The fifth is concerned with your personal development both inside and outside work, and the final section looks at the big picture.

Successful executives help their organizations to be more

effective too. As they put more into their firms, they gradually get more out in salary, status and satisfaction.

Companies prize executives who are effective and cast aside those who are not, so executives depend upon their effectiveness for their livelihood. Is business effectiveness something that most companies currently teach? I don't think so. Most executives are expected to learn on the job through trial and error, but this isn't always the most effective way to learn.

Why aren't we all effective all of the time? It's harder to be effective. It requires more awareness, will, and skills, but it is much more rewarding. When you are effective you bring into being that which you intended, you have the effect you wanted to have. You can help the people around you to be more successful too. You can set a powerful example. Your good habits can rub off on them just as an unsuccessful executive's bad habits tend to rub off on people too.

This book is a partnership between you and me. It works when we are on the same wavelength and you see something new. Do answer the questions in the Self Checks. They are about you: you are the subject, you are in charge. Have a pen, pencil or highlighter handy as you read. It's better to get insights than keep a pristine copy. Who would you save it for? So use the margins to make notes and mark the sections that you think you want to revisit, or use 'Post it' notes. One executive had a set of highlighter pens as well as his own copy of the document we were going to review. He marked what he agreed with in one colour, action points in another and so on. I felt underprepared as I had no such pens with me. By the time we finished reviewing the document, he had a set of highlighted notes and knew what he wanted to do while I had hardly started. Now there's an easy to copy habit.

Self Check

1. Why aren't we all effective all of the time?
2. What makes a successful executive?
3. What do you want to get out of this book?
4. Are you willing to change the way you work?
5. Are you willing to work at becoming more successful?
6. Are you ready to read the next section?

1.2 Brave new executive

We are entering the age of self-management

Whether working in large, medium or small enterprises, in commerce or for central and local government, today's executives mainly have to manage themselves. Because more and more executives report to each manager, that manager spends less and less time with each of them.

Yesterday's authority-based hierarchical environment, where everyone did as they were told, is disappearing. Communications technology allows information to be transferred up and down organizations at great speed, minimizing the need for lots of intervening layers of management, and making it easier for lots of people to report directly to one person. That's why organizations are delayering. In today's flatter organizations executives have to use initiative and judgement. Routine jobs are being done by that master of the routine, the computer. Who will pay someone to add up or organize information that could be sorted more quickly by a machine? This is why there's no place left for executives who simply take orders. Today's executives need to work out what to do for themselves, and management of others becomes occasional as we enter the age of self-management.

Everyone in an organization can be inundated with information, but who understands the whole situation? The need to understand the whole is one reason why big, single discipline departments, where everyone does the same thing, are breaking down. When financial people understood finance, operations people understood operations, marketing understood marketing, etc., only the people at the top – if anybody – understood the whole thing. Only they needed to, because only they needed to take initiatives. Today's communication technology can process single discipline information instantly, yet it doesn't provide any understanding of what's going on, just fragmentary snapshots. The hard bit is knitting together the different disciplines so you can see the whole picture and then take correct action. By all means, have an area of special knowledge but be a generalist too.

That's why multi-disciplinary teams are replacing inward-looking departments, and technology helps managers to monitor each team's performance. Quiet jobs are disappearing. Everyone's on the level, and there's not much more than one level.

You don't get by on years served or on seniority. However, this doesn't mean that youth always comes out on top. Judgement is vital, and experience can inform judgement. Your skills are vital to you because the skill-less are slipping from the executive scene ever more quickly. If you aren't up to it, you are likely to drop out of it.

So, every executive must help to define tasks as well as execute them. As local team members we set the standards which we strive to meet. We work with people, computers and phones; buy and sell and negotiate with clients and customers, suppliers and colleagues; exert and receive pressure; all without minute to minute supervision. We are expected to get on with it, and we do.

We take briefs from one another. We select work from our screen, on the phone and in meeting rooms. We produce and issue our own documents and print, fax and e-mail them. We present our work and follow it up. We see our own projects through while reporting intermittently. Indeed, as much as we report to others, team members report to us from below or beside or both. We brief them, guide them and review their work, and we do our best to get on with them all.

Executives must be more than executors. We can anticipate what needs to be done before it needs to be done. We can move a step ahead when we set our own agenda. We know our territory and others' too, and understand how our work fits in to a broader process. We can see when things are going well and notice when something is beginning to go wrong. We can be crisis preventers. We take initiatives, we spot better ways of doing things, and we can measure our own success. We can see whether our behaviour had the effect we had in mind. To a lesser extent, we can see when others are effective too, just as your boss and peers notice whether you seem to be effective.

While we are supposed to run things, it often feels, however, that we are given the run around, like tennis balls hit from one side of the net to the other – and no one ever asks a tennis ball for a point of view. You need to learn to wield a racquet.

New methods, markets and technologies constantly allow new ways to do things. We can change the way we work. We can affect the way other people work too, and these need not be one-off changes. They can be part of a rapid evolutionary process.

1.3 Successful people change the world

The main thing an executive needs to know is how to be a successful executive

Did you come into this world in order to leave it the way that it is? Or simply to earn a crust? Successful people change the world, or part of it, in the ways they intend. They choose what to do, they do it, and they see that it works. When it doesn't work, they change their behaviour and try again. For your part, you are successful when you work out what you want to do and you do it well.

Success is more than efficiency. You can do the wrong things efficiently, and so be efficient without being successful. You can go round in circles ever so efficiently without succeeding at anything. The differences are in awareness, skill and control. Successful executives work out what to do, take action and monitor results. We can all be successful executives more of the time.

5

The key to changing the world is changing yourself. In every industry there's an evolving body of knowledge to be discovered, in every discipline there are more practices and processes to be understood, but the main thing an executive needs to know is how to be a successful executive. It's that basic.

1.4 Have clear goals

Your goals can motivate you powerfully

If you don't know what you are about, who does? If you don't know what you want to achieve, how much will you achieve? The fact that you are reading this book suggests that you would like to be, or continue to be, successful.

What moves the world? The weather can affect people's moods, but it isn't the prime mover. So what does move the world? The truth is that effective people move the world. Why don't most people affect much of the world? What limits them? Some think they are limited by their genetic make-up. Your genes provide a starting point, but they don't stop you from changing as you go through the world. We needn't be prisoners of our genes. Your parents and others can have a powerful influence on you while you are still a child, offsetting or reinforcing the genetic make-up; so will your education, or lack of it, and other people affect you when you are an adult. It can be helpful to understand these influences, but you don't need to be imprisoned by them, and none of them need stop you changing yourself. You can exert an influence which far outweighs genes and education, parents and other adults. You can take charge of yourself.

How do people affect the world? To affect the world deliberately you must decide what you want, envisage the outcome you intend to bring about, and then commit yourself to achieving it. You must use your willpower and then take action.

What motivates you? You may decide you will be a brilliant executive so that your employer will want to give you a 30 per cent rise in salary at the next review. Some years ago, this was one of my main goals. I projected my salary growth year by year on a simple bar chart. Sure enough, the projections were fulfilled, but only because I also committed myself to giving my best day in day out. Financial goals might be important to you. Your skills are crucial so you might want to develop them in a particular way this year. You may have goals for each of your projects.

People tend to hit what they aim for. This applies to the golfer standing on the tee whose eye is taken by the bunker, as much as to the person who dreams of setting up a new company. My experience is that you get exactly what you aim for. The golfer hits the bunker. The entrepreneur sets up the company. A story is told of a Greek goddess who wanted to marry a mortal and wished that the mortal would be given eternal life so that they could live together forever. She got her wish – but on her timescale he aged very fast and so she was left forever married to an ancient husband. A poorly specified goal can bring disaster on the wisher. Do be sure about what you aim for; you may get it.

Some people aim to be rich. Given enough commitment, they normally achieve it – only to find that baubles mean little in themselves. The process of becoming rich was the principal reward; the aftermath is a disappointment. Sometimes people aim for mutually exclusive things, and often they aim for nothing in particular. Or they aim for the end without willing the means and so make little progress. Or they will the means but are unclear about their ends and fire off in different directions. You can be clear about means and ends.

Begin by working out what you want to achieve. Some people aim to achieve great goals in very short periods of time, but seldom succeed. Bearing in mind that the long term *begins* now, you can aim for long-term speed. Define clear goals in advance because you know this is the first step to achieving them. A particular outcome is more likely to be realized if it's a goal than if it's not. Besides, you like to know what you are working towards. If you don't feel motivated, you have not found motivating goals.

By all means begin by setting yourself small goals. If you

have never done so, set yourself the smallest reasonable goals for next week and slightly, but only slightly, bigger ones for next month. Make them so small that you know you can achieve them with a bit of effort. You may be surprised quite how much satisfaction you can get from achieving even little goals if you haven't achieved them before. As you get yourself into the habit of achieving goals, your confidence in your self grows, your expectations grow and you can make the goals a little bigger.

Imagine you have never done the high jump before and you set the bar to jump six feet this month. Would you manage it? Probably not. But suppose you decide to do four feet. (Even start at three foot six?) Might you manage that? And once you get into the habit of jumping that lower bar successfully again and again, might you not gradually jump a bit higher, and then higher still? You see, it isn't the goals themselves that are so important, but your ability to achieve them. It's the habit of achieving goals that defines success.

Self Check

1. Would you be more likely to achieve things if you aimed for them?
2. What really motivates you?
3. What are your main goals?
4. Does it matter to you if you don't achieve them?
5. Does it matter to you if you don't achieve anything?
6. What do you want to achieve today? this month? this year?
7. Can you make your short-term goals sufficiently small?
8. What are your main financial goals for your team?
9. What are your main financial goals for yourself?
10. What are your main goals for your current work?

1.5 Succeed

You start with your agenda

Success is a self-discipline. It can be accessed, absorbed and acted upon. When you decide that you *will* be successful your willpower starts to root for you, instead of sitting idly by. Many people don't succeed for the simple reason that they are scared of failing. Instead, they don't even try. At least they can comfort themselves with the thought that they might not have failed!

You are proactive, which means you set yourself tasks. You anticipate, you don't wait for other people to demand things, although you are likely to respond to their requests. So many people lose time managing the people who are chasing them for the things they haven't quite delivered, because they are so busy handling such requests! You take charge of what needs to be done because you identify what needs to be done and you act upon that information. You don't hide from the world, you are ready to jump right into it.

You use similar skills even when other people ask you to act. Whatever you are asked to do, you think about what could be achieved. It may be more or less than what has been asked for, or something quite different. You use your own judgement. Even when you supply what's been asked for, you may do it in a new way that hasn't been suggested. Make sure you understand the tasks set by others, and determine to meet the challenges they set too.

Fundamentally, you start with your own agenda, which helps to motivate you. The work you do for others becomes part of your agenda when you agree to do it. When you haven't worked out an agenda for a day, a week, a job, make some time available to consider your purposes, and put them in sequence. Starting with your agenda helps you to choose the way you do your work rather than letting others' goals fill your void.

Once you have decided to do something, you commit yourself to achieving your goal. You aren't put off by unanticipated difficulties or a negative mood. How much energy do we waste by beginning tasks which we never finish? Every time you don't finish something you started, you weaken your own trust in yourself. Become a task-completer.

Think of something you want to do. Shut your eyes and literally see happening what you intend, even though it hasn't happened yet in the real world. Envisage it again and again. See the detail. Now, can you feel just a bit more confidence? Can you feel the awakening of a seed of faith? Envisioning is powerful, so be careful what you envisage. Ponder the wrong thing and it's all too likely to come true.

In your eyes, there should be no such thing as 'failure', only a missed opportunity. The real failure, if it ever comes, is in failing to try again. A setback is only a problem if you don't come forward again. So the problem isn't encountering a defeat, it is *accepting* defeat. Try again, using what you learnt to avoid a similar result. Every 'failure' is a chance to learn, so take these chances as they come, however unwelcome they may seem.

If you want to find people who will succeed, look amongst the people who have also failed (although some highly successful people don't publicize previous failures). If you want to find people who will never succeed, find people who have never failed. They'll never take the risks that success requires. Success and 'failure' are two sides of the coin. Is that your kind of coinage?

How often do people 'fail'? How much more often do they fail to see and grasp the opportunity? The truth is we miss opportunities every day of the week. The solutions to most of our problems stare us in the face and we miss them, day in and day out. You can become opportunity minded. 'Failure' may be no more than a painful step on the path to success.

Self Check

1. How successful do you want to be?
2. Who is responsible for your success?
3. What would success in your work be to you?
4. How can you be successful in your work?
5. What would success mean in the rest of your life?
6. Do you complete the tasks others set you?
7. Do you do what you promise yourself you will do?
8. How much more successful can you be by working more?
9. How can you increase your effectiveness when you are working?
10. Can you envisage yourself achieving an important goal?

1.6 The five 'A's executive

Successful executives have learnt what it takes to be successful

There's more to being successful than thinking about it. What are the ingredients?

Unless you apply yourself, you will never achieve anything. So activity is a prerequisite for success. In some circumstances, the more you apply yourself, the more you may achieve. You might imagine that

Achievement = Application

This may be incomplete. However active you are, if you haven't acquired the necessary ability you still don't achieve anything. A better model may be

Achievement = Application + Ability

In other words, achievement is a function of application *and* ability. On further thought this is incomplete too. You can have the necessary ability, but if you don't have an adequate awareness of what is going on, you may fail. So

Achievement = Application + Ability + Awareness

To which we might also add the wonderful skill, demonstrated in sport as much as in organizations, anticipation. That's the quality that gets people in the right place at the right time with the right tools. In short

Achievement = Application + Ability + Awareness + Anticipation

which may be roughly right. This handbook deals with all five 'A's: application, which may be encouraged; ability, which may be developed; awareness, which grows through understanding situations and people; anticipation, which can be cultivated; and achievement, which is a synonym, more or less for success. You can become a five 'A's executive.

Self Check

1. What are your success factors?
2. Are you committed to developing each of them?
3. Can you develop self-awareness?
4. Do you notice your own attitude towards circumstances?
5. What would stop you from becoming a five 'A's executive?

1.7 Enjoy work

Smile and the organization smiles with you

I was once employed on a building site where I swept the dust and the quickly accumulating mud out of each freshly constructed house. As I brushed energetically to and fro, a labourer who had been there rather longer than me turned with a quizzical look and said, 'You enjoy work, don't you?' He had worked out what he needed to do to get paid, no more, no less. To judge from his reaction, he didn't enjoy his work, but you can enjoy almost any work you do, from speaking to sweeping.

Smile and the organization smiles with you. Frown and the same applies. You don't have to let your workplace affect your moods, although it might, and you don't need to depend upon it for your happiness which is sourced from inside you. In fact, rather than be affected by it, you can exert a powerful influence on your workplace. You can choose to be happy however daunting the circumstances around you because happiness is an internal state of being, it is how *you* are. Nothing and nobody can make you unhappy, although you may crack under adverse pressure. You can choose your response to the circumstances that surround you. If a colleague lets you down, you can respond by thinking, 'Oh no, this is too bad,' or you can look on it as an opportunity to retrieve a difficult situation. Every time, *you* choose your response. No one else can stop you enjoying your work.

Self Check

1. How much do you enjoy your work?
2. Can you be happy even when those around you aren't?
3. Can you be emotionally independent?
4. Have you noticed your performance when you are happy?
5. Have you noticed your performance when you are unhappy?
6. Do you let others get you down?
7. Are your good habits likely to rub off on others?
8. How much satisfaction can you get from doing work well?

1.8 Have a positive mental attitude

Mind precedes matter, ideas precede items

I introduced myself to a lady and asked, 'How are things?'

'Terrible,' she replied, with a shake of the head. I said I was sorry to hear that and asked her what was terrible. 'Everything,' she said, 'Everything is terrible.' I asked her to name something specific that was terrible. She couldn't. It was just 'everything' – she blamed The Government. She's not alone. The problem with pessimism is it's discouraging, and blaming someone else is disempowering. If it's the government's fault only the government can fix it; you can do nothing. The attitude has disempowered you. The reality is that no one is disempowered except those who think they are.

The successful executive tends to believe that things can be done. Otherwise nothing would ever get done. That doesn't mean you should vaguely think all sorts of things will happen without any planning or effort. Just simply think that they can be achieved with the right planning and effort. The future is an opportunity waiting to happen.

The phrase 'Perish the thought!' acknowledges the power of negative thinking. Everything needs to be created in the mind before it can be made in the world. Mind precedes matter. The internal world causes things to come into effect, and is then, in turn, influenced by the external world. Think it through and make it happen.

Ideas may surface when they are half formed in the mind. You may be roughly right, partly wrong and the thought may be incomplete, but don't kill ideas just because they aren't yet perfect. Instead, nurture them. When you come across a half-baked idea, look for ways to complete the baking. Particularly if you have made time to develop the right culinary skills.

We don't need to be unnecessarily critical of others, nor be too hard on ourselves. People, too, are like some ideas – partly right, partly wrong and incomplete. One sign of maturity is recognizing that we aren't perfect and we aren't going to become perfect tomorrow, but it's still worth working on it. In the meantime, accentuate the positive and eliminate the negative.

The fact that you don't know how to do something needn't put you off trying. If you already knew, there would be no challenge, and no challenge means no pay off. How often do you hear people saying, 'I can't do it.' How do they know? I suggest that they don't, but they paralyse themselves with their thinking. Even a toddler knows you have to get back up every time you fall over. Sooner or later you can walk. Whatever the task, you could look for, and ultimately find, ways to do it.

Our language reflects our thinking and also influences it, and you don't need to be into mantras to know that our words help to condition our minds. Use positive language when you communicate with others too. This isn't simply a matter of semantics. People find it easier to absorb positive language. If I say, 'Don't read the next paragraph until you have understood the point of this one', your mind has to think about the positive thing – reading the next paragraph – in order to work out what it is that you are not supposed to do.

All very complicated. I could express the same thought more positively by saying, 'Do make sure you understand the point of this paragraph before you go on to the next one', without a negative acoustic. Even more difficult are double negatives like 'Do not read the next paragraph if you haven't understood the point of this one.' What will *you* read next?

The successful executive is happy when coming across a new kind of challenge. Things we haven't done before are opportunities to stretch ourselves in new ways. Are you scared to stretch? When we do, we may uncover new skills. Ultimately, the routine tasks that we have done so many times before can get a bit dull. We thrive on difficulty.

The successful executive is enthusiastic. Enthusiasm can make the difference to any project's success because it affects the way that everyone looks at the project and the way they feel about their work. Enthusiasm isn't blind to the possibility of pitfalls. The successful executive will look out for dead-ends and attempt to avert them in good time.

A positive mental attitude tends to make you opportunity oriented. Fortune favours the bold. You look forward to the future, you can be naturally optimistic, and you know you can make a difference.

Self Check

> 1. Do you take a positive approach to your work?
> 2. Do you encourage others in their work?
> 3. Do you support new ideas?
> 4. Are you critical of others?
> 5. Do you use positive language?
> 6. Do you look forward to new challenges?
> 7. Are you put off when something new comes up?

1.9 Build relationships

If you sit on people, they behave like furniture

Successful executives don't work people, they work with people. In the post-industrial age, machines are usually taken for granted while people are the producers. You will find that people produce through their imagination and memory, eyes and ears, hearts and minds.

When two people work together three things determine the quality of the work. The ability of the first person, the ability of the second person, and the quality of the relationship. One and one makes three (the 'and' being the third item). That's synergy.

You need trust and courage to create a synergistic relationship. You need trust to be open to the other person and you need courage to be open to change. Are you willing to have your mind changed?

Mostly executives work with people they can see, but we can also build trust with people we only hear. I once worked with a woman who worked at a newspaper. We talked on the phone almost every working day for a year or so before we ever met and built a strong relationship even though neither knew what the other looked like. A colleague worked successfully with a client for four years before meeting. You can trust with your eyes shut. Sometimes executives just work with people electronically and it's possible to build a strong relationship even then. Just using words. Before the creation of the telephone and the aeroplane, many people interacted with one another only by post!

Even if you spend much of your time in front of a screen, the odds are someone gave you the brief, someone will review your work, and you will regularly meet with at least one other person.

Successful executives know their own performance depends partly upon others' performance, so the successful executive motivates those others to produce their best work. That means seeing things from their point of view, simply to avoid de-motivating them.

Good team work is much easier when there is trust between team members. You need the trust before you get to the good work. You can like someone without trusting them – they may amuse you, but would they always be straight with you or anyone else? Trust is hard to get and worth a great deal.

A successful executive works to earn each colleague's trust. To get it, refrain from gossip and criticism, however much of it you hear. A good rule is never to say behind someone's back what you wouldn't say to their face. Just imagine that they are present before you speak. You may be amazed the effect it has on you. Gossip can harm people and relationships. You can build trust by speaking up for people when they aren't around. In doing so, you cut across the criticism. Anyway, it shows respect for people. They'll count on you to stick up for them when they aren't around, and you will.

Think of the best work you have produced. How did it come about? Did you do it entirely on your own? Were other people involved? Was there a high level of trust between you? Was there a magic moment, or two, or more, a time when you could feel something being created?

Like good wine, relationships can improve over time. Unlike wine, they need never go off. You can build your network of contacts, year in year out. Your contacts may or may not be your friends. They may or may not overlap with your private life – you might choose to keep the two boxes separate – but your contacts are people you know you can work with well. You probably think they are good at their job and they may think the same about you, which provides some basic reliability. You have probably learnt to listen to each other, which provides the basis for mutual understanding.

If you stay within an organization, many of the people you now know may be your colleagues in ten years' time. You may have been through a lot together by then. You may be willing to go through a lot more for one another in future. If you move around within an industry, many of today's contacts may be tomorrow's clients and suppliers, as well as colleagues.

You might ask, 'Why not simply rely on ability? Why rely on other people at all?' And yet, as we have discussed, executives must rely on other people. It's unavoidable. Relationships are part of the ability. Your 'and' in the 'one and one' is part of the equation. It's not so much a matter of who you know, but of who knows your worth.

Almost everyone you meet could help you at some time and you could help them too. What's more, they are all people you could learn something from. They can increase your effectiveness no end. If you build goodwill with one new person per week, your contacts would exceed one hundred people in two years. That's some network. And you never know who will do quite what in your network. I once worked at a firm for a manager, left the firm but agreed to return to it later, and became the manager's manager – but our relationship was still good.

One of the ways to build relationships is to work well with people: just to be civil when you are working with them. Sometimes, when I've worked with people who are junior to me, I've been relatively brief with them. I've explained the task as quickly as I can and discouraged any questions by letting them know that I expect them to have understood. Guess what happened. I saved time at the outset, but I lost time later on when the task wasn't done so well. And then those people weren't so keen to get another task from me in future. The light in their eyes was a bit dimmer. If you treat people like furniture, they behave like furniture. Inert.

Make sure you are courteous to people even when convention doesn't require it. Juniors notice it. They get treated brusquely much of the time. Then you come along and treat them well. Guess what happens. They want to work with you. Nothing is too much trouble. They will come through for you because they feel you care about them. The same applies to secretaries. Behave well to Personal Assistants and you will probably find their bosses are better informed about you. How can the ill mannered compete with the courteous? It may be tough to be tender, but it's worth it every time.

Self Check

1. Do you work with people, not just merely beside them?
2. How good are your relationships with those around you?
3. How civil are you towards them?
4. When things go wrong, is it always one of your colleagues' fault?
5. Do you seldom see it as your own fault?
6. How do you want them to think of you?
7. How well do you know their strengths and weaknesses?
8. Which of their strengths do you think you could learn from?
9. Which are the most effective executives you have worked with?
10. Which of their habits could you build in to your routine?
11. Do you keep in touch with the good people you have worked with?
12. Are you building your network of contacts?

1.10 Master the basics

We need to adjust our vision if we want to see more clearly

However high you rise, life is still mainly a matter of doing the basic things well, and helping others to do them well. In fact, the higher you rise, the more opportunities you get to deal with the really basic things – with the causes, not just their effects.

19

There is one person in this world over whom you could exercise a huge influence. You. Most of all, you should build an outstanding working relationship with yourself. Everybody's different. So find the best ways to work with yourself, the kinds of task you can do best and the roles at which you excel. Then look for those roles.

Try to find the times of day when you do different kinds of work best, the way you assimilate information most effectively and the kinds of preparatory work that yield the highest dividends for you. Learning these things can make a massive difference to your effectiveness. You can be a better manager of yourself than your own manager! You can take total responsibility for your own performance.

As an executive, you may spend time rushing around trying to get routine things done. You can feel like a tennis ball that's thrashed from racquet to racquet until you are hit into the net or off the court. Your challenge is to make time to learn what to do and to do it better. As you do so, you create more time for yourself.

Every executive is confronted with problems. Complex problems can be simple to solve, and simple ones can be intractable. Either way, problems may challenge and involve you. Be careful, you may get so wrapped up in the problem you stop searching for the solution. The problem, being known, may be more comfortable than the solution, being unknown. You find yourself aimlessly wandering round and round a problem. If you start by identifying the solution, you may find the problem, and its solution, become much clearer. Properly defining the problem may take you most of the way to the solution. The simple solutions are usually hardest to find because they are right in front of your nose. When we don't notice them, we need to adjust our vision.

Some executives focus on complex and involving problems. You may hear them say 'That's interesting,' to an unusual situation as though it might not otherwise have interested them at all. Isn't interest a prerequisite for doing business? I often hear people say, 'That's exciting!' as though there is value in excitement – there isn't. You can't bank excitement. Anyway, excited people seldom make good decisions. Temporarily, they are just a little bit unstable.

20

A colleague I once worked with was almost always excited and nervy. He would spread ripples of panic wherever he went. Meetings he participated in were strangers to reflective thought.

Effectiveness is mainly a matter of performing well at a basic level. Of dealing well with situations that crop up again and again. Think of the situations that regularly recur in your work. Focus on doing them well and you will start to move ahead.

These days computer skills are part of an executive's basic repertoire. Without them, your career may be perilously short. So there's another basic to acquire.

Self Check

1. How well have you mastered all of the basics?
2. How well will you work if you can't do the basics well?
3. Do you take time to understand how things work?
4. Do you attend to detail?
5. Will others attend to detail on your work if they see that you don't?
6. How effective do you look to others when they see you can't do basic things?
7. How are you improving your computer skills?

1.11 Be reliable

Reliability is the real litmus test

The second most valuable basic organizational quality is the ability to do what you agree to do, to make your actions conform to your words, and do what you say. It's as simple as that, and as appreciated too.

You may know immediately, from the look in their eyes, whether someone believes you will do what you have just agreed to do. The low look says it all.

You might say, 'Hey, what does he mean? Don't we all do

what we say we will do?' Unfortunately not. When was the last time you said you would do something and didn't quite get it done for whatever 'reason'?

Or maybe it was a commitment to yourself. You looked at something and realised that you needed to do something about it, but you haven't got around to it for days, weeks, months. It's still there waiting to be done.

Maybe something got in the way. You said you would do it but you couldn't stop something else coming up, which you hadn't anticipated. While we can't anticipate every particular thing, we can anticipate that things will come up – it's in the nature of executive life – and make allowances for this when we make commitments. Give yourself an amnesty. Re-negotiate the previous commitments that you made when you didn't always follow through. Start over and only commit to what you definitely will do.

An associate approaches this task the other way around and gets the same results. She conforms her words to what she knows she can do. She reflects before she makes a commitment. Then, and only then, she's as good as her word.

Managers will choose reliable people over unreliable people for almost any useful task. While working with reliable people is a joy, working with unreliable people can be a nightmare. They tell you one thing, and then do another, or don't do anything at all. You can't rely on them to complete your work. It's hit and miss. I've encountered such people; sometimes I've even been one.

In time, reliable people get to work on the more interesting projects and they tend to get promoted fast too, while unreliable people are shuffled towards the exit door. One of the worst situations to be in is where a whole team has become unreliable. Nobody is following through in the way that they should. Everyone is pretending, everyone is covering up, nobody means it. Ultimately, the whole team, division or company is brought out into the light and discovered.

Why don't we always manage to do what we say we will do? Sometimes we agree to take on a task that really is beyond us. Occasionally, we take on a job that is within our ability but we accept an impossible timescale. Sometimes we make promises to please, only to disappoint.

More often, we let ourselves down in the execution or lack of it. We just don't deliver with enough thought and planning, or quality in the work. We don't try hard enough early enough and then we scramble around at the last minute and produce some poor work because there isn't enough time left to do a quality job.

We don't really commit ourselves to achieving the task. We don't get on top of it. It gets on top of us. At some point, the difficulty, inconvenience or frustration becomes too much and we settle for non-performance, or the deadline becomes too real to ignore and we finally spur ourselves into action.

We may compound our difficulty by trying to gloss over our failure. We probably try to hide it from ourselves, let alone others – 'It wasn't my fault. Someone else let me down. It was his fault.' In doing so, we disempower ourselves. Sooner or later our errors emerge, and the quieter we have been the bigger the risk of an explosion. A controlled explosion tends to work better. It gets the error off your chest. What's more, it builds trust. People feel they know where they are with you. You don't hide things from them. You admit your mistakes without dwelling on them. The world didn't end and you moved on.

Sometimes our short-term mood, whim or craving overpowers our longer-term goal. We give in, it wins, we lose. Probably, we didn't really commit ourselves to achieving the goal. Maybe we didn't really think we would do it. Perhaps our will had been sapped by previous failures of a similar kind, or worse still, we never thought we would do it when we made the commitment.

Or maybe we agreed to do the work but we don't actually want to do it because we think it's really beneath our status. We ensnared ourselves. We set ourselves up for conflict.

Of course, we all fail sometimes, but if you regularly let others down, you create big problems for yourself. Your relations with others will deteriorate, and your own sense of integrity will weaken.

How can you begin to become more reliable? Start by making and keeping promises to yourself. You may need to start with small promises that you know you can keep if you try and then move on to slightly larger ones. Once you get into a habit of keeping commitments to yourself you will find it equally natural to keep promises to other people too. But if you don't keep promises to yourself, you are at the whim of your moods. Every promise you keep builds your sense of integrity.

Some people only really start to work when it's the eleventh hour. You might think that up until that point they don't find the task sufficiently challenging, or they don't want to produce their work until it will be too late for anyone else to change it. More often, the pain involved in doing the work seems to outweigh the pain involved in taking it easy until the consequences of failing to do the work become sufficiently real, and action ensues. Some enjoy last minute crises. That's why they don't do things until they are urgent. They are urgency addicts who actually enjoy the dramas that ensue. It gives them a chance to be centre stage. While coaching soccer I have noticed that a misbehaving boy will sometimes fail to return a football and draw out the moment even though all eyes are upon him. He's enjoying the attention. Dramas provide a sense of self-worth and help people to feel valued. Without these drama-seekers' input there would be catastrophe left, right and centre, but the possibility that they could have prevented the crisis from ever occurring may be overlooked.

Urgency addiction is so much easier than being self-disciplined. Self-discipline requires your voluntary effort. It's the clearest signal of a successful person. By failing to get organized in good time, urgency addicts accumulate so many urgent things which must be done that they definitely don't have time for non-urgent tasks like learning how to organize their time. I gave one over-pressured urgency addict a short book about delegation. A year later, I asked for it back, but he still hadn't found the time to look at it, let alone read it, and it showed in his department. His people are busy, they feel pressured, wanted and important, but they are failing and they know it.

Urgency addicts are dangerous to the people around them and themselves. Sooner or later, their last-minute efforts are insufficient. Something goes wrong and they miss the target. Even those of us who do have some self-discipline sail close to the rocks when we aim to do things on time rather than within time. By aiming to do things on time, you lay yourself open to a last-minute hitch moving you off course, and then you are late, whatever you do. However, if you aim to get things done in good time, you reduce the cost of last-minute delays, and avoid panics and time-related failures. The effective executive does things *in* time not *on* time by getting things done *before* they need to be done. Don't work to deadlines. Work within 'livelines'.

You might think that delivering things right on the deadline gives your supervisor less time to criticize your work. That seems a cowardly way to work. Why not get others' input? True, they may change your work, but how else will you discover how to produce better work next time and thereafter?

Getting things done in good time brings another advantage. Unforeseen events rarely reduce you to a state of panic. You are calm when events put you under pressure because you have left yourself sufficient room for manoeuvre.

Self Check

1. Do you want to be a reliable person?
2. Do you want others to think of you as reliable?
3. Can you make and keep a promise to yourself?
4. Will you be more effective if others are willing to rely on you?
5. Do you aim to get things done on time or in time?
6. Do you feel better or worse when you get things done in good time?
7. Will you save time by putting off getting started?

1.12 Think things through

You can think deeply even while you sleep

You may feel you are so busy that you spare little or no time

25

to think deeply about what you are doing. You may not find time to define clearly the problems that confront you and to probe deeply for possible solutions.

If you can, start with the solution you want to realize. Then state the problem clearly: the thing that may stop you from achieving the solution. If you don't identify the problem you are unlikely to come up with a way to create the solution. It doesn't matter that you may not know how to solve the problem. Indeed, if you knew how, you wouldn't need to think. The exercise is almost invariably fruitless if you decide in advance that you can't find the answer. Try deciding you can and see if you notice any differences as you allow your mind to search for solutions. Stating the problem in the form of a question can make it more dynamic and prompt your mind to come up with an answer.

Having a rudimentary understanding of logic helps you to think clearly. At its simplest, logic is a matter of combining two or more ideas, which when used in this context are called premises, and which if taken together lead necessarily to a conclusion. For instance, if it is true that Smith's is a business and that all businesses have income then it necessarily follows that Smith's has income. This is called a syllogism. It's the basic construction of logic. On the other hand, if Smith's is a business but some businesses don't generate any income at all, then Smith's may have no income. So something may be true even if it doesn't necessarily follow from the information you have. Obversely, even if something necessarily follows from two or more premises, it may not be true if either of the premises is untrue. Smith's may be a non-trading company.

Perhaps the most common logical fallacy is to confuse an 'is' with an 'ought'. Something may or may not be so, but neither state means that it ought to be so. And whether or not a thing ought to be so, it may or may not exist.

One way to think deeply is to lay out your problems before you go to sleep at night. You can think while you sleep. I am convinced this is what is meant by the fairy tale about The Elves and the Shoemaker. You may recall that an impoverished shoemaker cut out the pieces of leather for his last pair of shoes before going to bed one night and woke up to find a beautiful pair of shoes ready in the morning. The 'elves' had made it for him. I think the elves are a metaphor for the subconscious mind. If you haven't already done so, try it yourself. Make sure you assemble all the relevant material or you will finish with incomplete shoes! Don't try to get the results before you go to bed. Just ask for them in the morning, as directly as you like. Your subconscious can work all night long without even disturbing you for a moment, and the results can be stupendous.

Try reviewing your schedule at night and focus on the main thing you have to do tomorrow. Imagine yourself doing it well. You can give yourself a flying start to the week by reviewing your weekly schedule on a Sunday night and then turning in. Watch that work flow.

The best way to improve your ability to think is to practise thinking. Do it as people talk. Ask yourself, 'Is that right? Is that really true? Have they thought that through? What else would follow if that were true?'

Self Check

1. How much of your time do you spend thinking?
2. What do you do with your thoughts?
3. Do you ever forget a powerful thought?
4. Do you try to make sure that you write your thoughts down?
5. Do you keep a journal of your thoughts?
6. Do you try to assemble all relevant material before concentrating on the solution?
7. How quickly can you spot non-sequiturs and fallacies?

Chapter Two

Organize Yourself

Think of something you have been meaning to do for some time. It could be at work or at home. Consider how long it will take to complete. An hour, maybe two, or just five minutes? Think of anything you need to get in order to help you to do it, identify an early opportunity to do it and pencil it in your schedule. Doing things that you have decided to do increases your ability to get things done. Simply do what you say you will do.

2.1 Get prepared

Successful executives do tomorrow's work today

Some days, everything is thrown at you. It's non-stop. Just one thing after the other. You are stretched yet you still manage to cope. How? Other days you may not. What's the difference? The answer is that you coped because you were prepared.

Preparation applies to everything, from the state of your mind to the state of your files; from your attitude to yourself to your relations with others, and hence their willingness to give you help when you need it.

Think about the physical aspects of your work. If your disks and paper files are well organized, you can retrieve any information you need in a few minutes: the absence of something won't trip you up just when you need it. Every time you can't easily find something, you have to slow down – even stop – and your integrity takes a blow. You don't need to take those blows any more.

Get prepared. Don't let your handwritten notes drift all over the place because they are scrawled on bits of paper. Instead, keep them in a dated Day Book so you can reach them fast. If your phone list is up to date, you don't have to hunt for numbers. At one time I would regularly search for some numbers I needed. Each time I got the number, I scribbled it on a bit of paper and then hurried to make the call to try to make up time – which was fine until I needed to make the same call again. It's better to make one note somewhere permanent.

You can be familiar with all the firm's processes that you are likely to encounter. If they aren't in a manual, ask, 'How do we handle that?', 'What's our procedure for dealing with this?' If there is a procedure you will discover it. If there isn't, maybe it is time one was created.

Being well prepared means you are in good shape because you got enough sleep the night before and you are sticking to a reasonably healthy diet. You arrived at work in good time to execute the work you planned. You have structured all of your projects so that you have some flexibility. You will have thought about what you need to achieve today and can see in seconds which tasks can be shuffled on to another day and which won't wait. You know the limit to your flexibility so you can quickly recognize when you will want to seek more help.

Preparedness also includes organizing back-up for when you need it. You will already have good relations with your colleagues so that they are willing to consider giving you help when required. Also you will have a good enough record of delivering to your managers and clients so that they will understand if and when you have to say no.

You thought about the day in advance. You understand what is happening in each of the areas of your work. You can identify most of the likely problems so you anticipate them and nip them in the bud. As far as possible, you probably did the work you would need to do today, yesterday. Before it became a problem.

You like to solve problems. When things go wrong, you don't start jumping up and down, and you don't start to fear the worst either. You think about why they have gone wrong, what needs to be done now and how you could avoid the problem in future. Your preparedness helps you to stay calm.

Self Check

1. Can you lay your hands on anything you have filed in a minute or so?
2. Are you in good enough shape to step up a gear today if necessary?
3. Do you know what you have scheduled today?
4. Could you see which tasks you can move to another day?
5. How many of your colleagues would you help out if they asked you?
6. How many of your colleagues would help you out if you asked them?
7. What are the main kinds of problems that you encounter?
8. How could you prevent a recurrence?

2.2 Have bits and pieces handy

Successful executives have a place for everything and keep everything in its place

Successful executives sort all the humdrum aspects of their work so that they don't get in the way of bigger things.

You can lose time looking for the things you need again and again. Do you ever find you need a pen, pencil or pad, rubber, ruler or sharpener, envelope, notepaper or stamp? You stop your work to look for them. Once you have disrupted your rhythm, you may then go and interrupt others by asking them for something basic too. You advertise a low standard of efficiency. At some offices, finding a bit of notepaper, a calculator, or a sharpener, takes minutes.

Successful executives rarely spend time looking for things because they know where they are. They have a place for everything and they keep everything in its place. Use your desk and drawers for the things you need to have within reach, not the things you don't need regularly.

Pre-code your phone to speed dial your most frequently used numbers, if it will let you do so. Keep a phone list handy and create your own if you need to. Most phones have a panel you can use to display often-used numbers.

Don't clutter your desk with papers. Act on what you need to act on; pass on what you need to pass on; file what you don't need now but may need again; chuck the rest. Clutter might make you feel more comfortable but it advertises poor organization. Never put papers on the floor by your desk, or anywhere else on the floor. You have to work much harder to be efficient in the middle of clutter. You have to remember exactly where you put each item *because* there is no system, just piles of stuff.

For one thing, papers are merely a means to an end. Either you read the papers you get or you don't. If you don't read them, you might as well throw them away. Once you have read them, you either take action or you don't. If you do need to keep papers, you will want to keep them with the papers to which they relate.

How often have you found yourself unable to find a document? You can't remember where you put it? It's an unnecessary nightmare. Time spent thinking about where you put each document is time that you can't spend doing something useful, and lost time is irrecoverable. The solution is to run a system. I like to keep my desk clear, which seems to give me more room to think, and that's where most of the value is.

Keeping things handy gives you more power to achieve. It's all part of becoming a well-oiled machine.

If you haven't already done so, get in control of the little things. Experience the joy of being able to get what you need without trouble or fuss. Then you can make a bigger contribution.

Self Check

1. What are the things you need to do your work?
2. How many of them do you need to reach in a second or two?
3. Which of them do you need regularly?
4. What do you need in your desk?
5. What must you keep on your desk?
6. Is there anything you need to leave out on your desk overnight?

2.3 Use your diary

Successful executives always turn up

Have you ever failed to turn up for something because you forgot it? Or failed to give apologies in time, or double-booked yourself?

As soon as you get details of a meeting, check your diary or organizer. It may tell you that you can't get there, or that you need to re-arrange another meeting in order to do so. Write in the details. A pencil or keypad is more flexible than a pen, because then you can change your diary, when you need to, without crossing things through. Those pencils with erasers on the end are even better. You can rub out mistakes at once.

Write in the start time of the meeting and then the estimated finish time. If an end time wasn't volunteered, ask when's the latest time by which it will finish. Then write the name of the meeting, the venue and a phone number at which you could contact the organizer in case an emergency prevents you from being there.

If you think it will take you fifteen minutes to get to the place where you are meeting, write in a leaving time twenty-five minutes ahead of the start time. It's amazing how often people get 'stuck in traffic'. When you are late, you dissipate goodwill. The people you are meeting are less keen on you. Your chances of success have diminished before you have even started. The last time you were seriously late, how did the meeting go? If you've never been there before, check the whereabouts. Stick a map on top of the file.

Self Check

1. Do you write meetings into your diary as soon as you get the invite?
2. Do you capture the start and finish time and venue in your diary?
3. Do you get a contact phone number in case your plans change?
4. Do you set off an extra ten minutes early?
5. Do you make a habit of getting to your meetings in good time?
6. Do you always take the papers you need?

2.4 Control the flow

Successful executives process paper once

Do you ever find yourself coming back to the same bits of paper again and again?

Paper may pour down on you every week. Your in-tray may heave daily. Your computer may receive direct faxes and e-mail too. The time it takes to receive, note, read and file paper plus any e-mail could fill your day, before you achieve anything. Handling memos, letters and other documents efficiently and effectively is a substantial task.

You need to sort the important from the unimportant, the readable from the forgettable, the actionable from the fileable. Sorting the wheat from the chaff is vital. You can do one of four things with the written communication you receive: act on it; pass it to a colleague; file it for future reference; or bin it.

Don't leave post or internal mail unopened. Open it fast. There may be something that requires immediate attention.

The first decision you need to make is whether to give it any attention at all. That is, beyond the second or two that it takes you to scan it and make that decision. That's your opportunity to bin it without a second thought. You don't note it or even try to remember it. Now you have cut the size of the pile.

You need to scan the rest more carefully but you may not need to read it all, or even most of it. Your next decision is would some of it be better attended to by someone else? Maybe you can write a note on the top of the sheet asking that person to review it, act on it, do as they see fit, get back to you with their views, or whatever course of action seems to you to be appropriate. It's off your plate. You have passed it to them. If it's important that it is followed up, you may want to take a copy and put it in the file you keep of things that you give to them, or simply make a note that that person has the document.

Maybe scanning it tells you that you don't need to do anything or even know about it now, but you just might need it in future. Fine. Put it in the most appropriate file. If it doesn't fit within a particular file, create a new one; or maybe a more detailed look has told you that you can chuck it after all.

Now you are down to the papers which seem to need attention. You can decide which, if any, require immediate attention, and which can be slotted into your day at the time you choose. In either case, read them closely with a pencil to hand and make notes as you go along. Maybe someone has asked you for feedback. Notes in the margin may do perfectly. If you do them as you read, they will take you only a moment or two more than just reading it and doing nothing. After which you still have the written work to do. Get your response back as soon as you are satisfied with it, but think through what you want your associate to do with it, and what response you want. Don't sit on it for a day or two unless you must consult with others, or you will slow up the whole process. If it's internal, maybe you can drop it round to the office and stretch your legs at the same time. You need to be out and about, and it's probably quicker than the internal mail.

Sometimes you need to think about something more deeply before you respond. Put the thinking time into your schedule. Make sure you do it and then get back within the required time frame.

Sometimes you have to involve others. If it's a meeting you need, make sure you set it up fast – even though you may want to schedule it some way ahead so the necessary preparatory work is done – and start work preparing for the meeting. Maybe you begin by circulating a note about the purpose of the meeting and ask people to come along with a particular task completed. It could be a line or two.

If you can avoid it, don't leave papers unprocessed at the end of the day. Keep things moving. Don't become the glue in the system, the person who slows things down. If you cultivate a habit of dealing with things efficiently, you will gradually find that the people you deal with get a bit more efficient too, especially when it comes to dealing with your work. Efficiency breeds efficiency. If you do have outstanding papers to sort and act upon, keep them in one place and make time to get through them all. Don't let it hang over you.

So, process paper once. Review the material, decide what to do with it, do it and move on. Don't put it back in your tray unread, review it, put it back, pick it up again and so on. Check your tray now. What's in it? How much has been there for too long gathering dust? Can you make some time available to clear it today?

A good filing system enables you to retrieve material fast. There is no purpose whatever in filing away material *per se* because it's not what you put in that counts, it's what you can get out. A good system saves time because you don't spend time looking for things. It saves you energy too because you don't have to think about where you put things, which frees your mind for more creative tasks.

If you don't have a filing system which works for you, create one now. For this purpose, ignore the material you already have and think about the material you actually need to get your hands on, whether or not you already have it. You don't need to have any material at all to set up a filing system because the best time to set up a filing system is before you have any material to put in it. Shape your files to reflect your needs. Let them influence what you keep and what you do with it, rather than the other way around. Set up a proactive filing system.

Think about how your work is organized. What are the

main different kinds of work you do? How do they subdivide? What does it look like as a flow diagram? What material do you need to retrieve and when? The answers to these questions will help you shape your system.

Successful executives clear their desks every day. Why leave papers lying out on your desk? They might be read by passers-by or may fall off the desk and disappear. However, the main reason you shouldn't leave papers about on your desk is that mess clutters the mind, and you may want to keep your mind clear to think. Be on top of your paperwork, not underneath it.

Self Check

1. When do you deal with your paper and e-mail?
2. Do you open, note, action and file at once or take separate processes for each item?
3. How do you read documents?
4. When you've finished reading, do you know the key points?
5. Can you refer to them easily?
6. Do you use a highlighter pen as you read?
7. Do you make a note of action points as you finish reading?
8. How do you process the work you receive?
9. How do you deal with fax and post and e-mail?
10. How quickly can you access the material you need?
11. What does your filing system look like?
12. What material do you need to retrieve quickly?

2.5 Clarify each brief

Successful executives get good briefs

Even the most proactive executive has to respond to briefs and requests from colleagues. Executives are part of a team.

The quality of the work you produce depends crucially

on the quality of the briefs you receive. If it's not clear to you what needs to be accomplished, you are unlikely to do the right thing. If you don't have the right question, you won't produce the right answer. While a good brief doesn't guarantee good work, a bad brief positively invites bad work.

When someone asks you to do something you may be tempted to say OK without hesitation. They probably want you to say yes. You may both be short of time and you want to get on. Why try to make things difficult? But taking on unclear tasks plants trouble.

Make sure you understand a brief before you accept it. Focus on what, how much, when, who to? What is it that's really required? When does it need to be done? What form does the work need to take? What should your finished product look like? Where does it need to be sent? How much can you spend? Whose authority do you need? What do you need in writing before you start? Be clear about the quality too. If you accept a brief you don't understand, you create a problem, but get the brief right and the rest follows. Articulate your understanding of the brief to the person who gave it to you, to check you have the same understanding of what's required.

You may get to the point where you understand the brief but it still doesn't seem to be a sensible use of your time. Ask the person who gave you the brief to outline the purpose of the work. You may be missing something, or you may come up with a better idea.

Self Check

1. Do you accept tasks without knowing what's expected?
2. Do you listen closely when you are being given a task?
3. If you are being given an oral brief, do you make notes?
4. Do you try to establish exactly what's required?
5. Do you check when it's required and in what format?
6. Do you check where it's required?
7. Do you accept or seek to revise a bad brief?
8. Do you make notes as you get the answers?

2.6 Look, listen, learn

Successful executives make mistakes once

You don't need to make the same mistake twice. Looked at this way, each first-time 'mistake' is an opportunity to learn how to avoid making the same mistake again. The 'learning executive' is dynamic.

When things don't work well, you may get frustrated. Sometimes frustration is followed by regret, or blaming someone else, or a redoubling of effort to get the right outcome. But extra effort won't avoid a repetition of the failure if it wasn't lack of effort that caused the problem.

Scientists progress by carrying out experiments. They do something and see what happens, then they do the same thing and see if it happens again. Before long, they have a hypothesis about cause and effect. You can do the same.

If you find the same things happen to you over and over, it's probably because you are doing the same things in the same way. You're unlikely to find that repeating your behaviour produces a different outcome. If you're forever rushing around in the midst of one crisis or another, more crises will leap upon you tomorrow. If people constantly appear to let you down, they will probably go on doing so. If things seem to go wrong in your life, they will continue to do so. We are the unwitting authors of our circumstances. Nothing much will change in your life until you change your own behaviour.

You need to notice what you do, because that's what you are going to change, and then you can make the changes. These are two of the biggest challenges facing any executive.

It's possible to fail repeatedly and not learn anything from the experience, but experience can be a great teacher and failure can be the most powerful teacher of all. Most people fail before they succeed. I have failures, which is why I have successes. The same is likely to apply to you. Every failure contains the seeds of some future success, but seeds are only seeds. They need to be discovered, watered, fed, developed, before they will blossom. You will need to overcome discouragement with fresh courage.

One reason that it can be difficult to see what we do is that our eyes face outwards. We focus on other people. The main thing our eyes don't see is ourselves. Even when we do see ourselves in action, for example a video play-back of a training session, we tend to filter what we don't want to notice. Our perspective does not usually include ourselves.

Our ego feeds on praise and wilts under criticism. Somewhere within our psyche, we may suspect that we may not be quite as good as we think we are. Occasionally that repressed thought may break out in a feeling that we are useless, but most of the time the thought is kept under lock and key.

People who haven't failed at something can be danger-ous. They may be less aware of the circumstances which typically precede failure and have less understanding of its consequences. Watch first-timers piling into an 'ever upward' housing market before prices collapse. When people think a thing is bound to work, they stop thinking.

You can watch what happens and see what works. Life is a matter of trial, error and learning, and the most valuable of these is learning.

Self Check

1. Do you notice what happens when you take action?
2. Do you notice when things don't work?
3. Do you see how you could have avoided that?
4. Do you sometimes repeat the same mistakes?
5. Have you made time to reflect on your behaviour?
6. Can you begin to see how you would need to change?
7. Would you like to change the outcome?
8. Will you commit to changing your input?

2.7 Manage yourself

Success can become routine

You are the person who is best placed to manage yourself. No manager can spend lots of time organizing the executives who report in. The manager passes them the tasks, provides guidance on the process and evaluates the work. Most managers don't stand over executives' shoulders throughout. Most managers don't even suggest how executives should organize themselves. They expect them to learn it for themselves.

You can create any number of routines to increase your effectiveness. Once they are established, you can do them on auto-pilot. You don't have to think about them. Your mind is free to do more.

Routines provide routes. Imagine someone who has none. This executive lacks a map. Every task needs to be planned afresh. Each one needs to be thought through. Minutiae need to be carefully considered. Far from inhibiting freedom, routines create it.

What things do you need to do in the same way every day, every week, every month? How can you make them an automatic part of your schedule? Or someone else's? Can you make sure that you do them every time on time like clockwork? Factories are much more effective when they do the same thing over and over. You can treat some of your relatively mundane tasks in that way. Automate or delegate as much as you can.

What's the best way to begin your day? Does the day run more smoothly if you compile your task list before you start on the tasks themselves? Does what's happened overnight affect your day? Does your mail need attention as soon as it arrives or are there other more important things to do first? Do you need to make a daily report, and how soon can you prepare it?

Self Check

1. How well organized do you want to be?
2. Wouldn't it be brilliant if you were really well organized?
3. How much would it be worth for your life to run smoothly?
4. Who is best placed to organize you?
5. What systems do others use to be effective?
6. Which systems could you create to be more effective?
7. What tasks do you have to do again and again?
8. How could you turn them into routines which you do automatically?
9. What's the best way to begin your day?

2.8 Get things done

Above all, executives execute

The successful executive makes a habit of getting things done. If you commit yourself to doing it you must do it, even if you don't feel like it when the time comes. After a massive series of efforts, this becomes second nature. Failure is the exception to your rule.

Most people do things when the perceived benefits out-weigh the costs. People who simply think about the immediate assignment without noticing or appreciating the benefits of completing it are unlikely to start on the task, much less complete it. But the person who focuses on the results of the work will be motivated. The work is simply a means to an end, and if the end is a good one, and you keep it in mind, doing it won't be a problem; the burden gets lighter and you can become happy even as you are doing a troublesome chore of little obvious interest. You exercise a little self-discipline.

Even as we do what we have decided to do, our minds think thousands of thoughts. Every day, thoughts come and go. Ideas come up before us and move away. Many of them can be discarded but some of them are actionable ideas and some of them relate to specific tasks we should do or should already have done. These ideas come, as it were, free since they require no effort to generate. Actually, it seems to take more effort to stop the flow of thoughts.

The successful executive uses them when they are any good. He makes a note of the useful ideas and the work that he should follow through. Some people make a quick note on a yellow sticker, others go straight for their diaries or organizers, some simply memorize them. Once the note is made, your mind is free to move on to the next thought, and then the next.

Discipline is for yourself.

Self Check

1. Are you in the habit of getting things done?
2. Do you defer tasks until they are a problem?
3. Do you focus on the benefit of getting something done?
4. Is this as real to you as the process itself?
5. Do you make notes of what you've got to do?
6. If not, do you always remember all of your tasks?
7. Do you do so immediately the task comes to mind?
8. If you don't, do you always get the detail right?
9. Do you regularly refer back to your task list?
10. Do you tick or cross off jobs once they are done?

2.9 Buy wisely

Know what you want before you try to buy it

Executives command resources. When we are not reading or writing, talking or listening, or just plain thinking, we often buy or sell. And even when we are doing other things, we are still sometimes buying or selling.

Spending other people's money is the easiest thing in the world. It's fun. You buy things and you aren't worse off because your organization paid for everything. Spending wisely is much harder. Many executives are responsible for big budgets. Successful executives spend wisely.

There are lots of courses to help you to sell, but not so many to help you to buy. Buying well is a skill which some salespeople under-rate, perhaps because they think that passion and energy go into the selling but not into buying. A salesperson may sometimes fail through no fault, whereas all a buyer has to do is make a choice. Well, not quite. Buyers have to get it right.

Buyers have to make the right decision from amongst any number of possibilities, plus they need to get the right possibilities to choose from in the first place. This may mean researching a market as well as writing a brief which specifies what needs to be provided. At the outset, the buyer needs to know 'What do I want to buy?' The buyer must also be clear on the buying criteria. Is price important, and if so, to what extent? Is quality important, and if so, what does quality mean; and how would you know if it was there?

Buyers need to shape the buying process. Is there time to issue a 'Request For Information' ('RFI'), and would it help anyway? To how many parties should a written brief be issued, and is a written response the most appropriate next stage? Is there time for individual presentations, and if so how many of them?

The buyer also drives the timetable. When does the order need to be delivered? When must the order be issued? When must the brief be issued? How much time will it take competitors to respond?

Some buyers use the fact that they have the budget to take a superior position. Not to put too fine a point on it, they expect the salesperson to grovel to them, and some salespeople play up to buyers and encourage them to think they, the buyers, are somehow special, just because they have the bucks. This is an unnecessary distraction from the task at hand. The buyer and seller should be engaging in a common activity: finding the best product or service to suit the buyer's needs, on the most mutually advantageous terms. They are trying to help one another and the benefit of working this out should accrue to both parties. Sure, the salesperson may get a commission, but could the service provide a benefit to the purchaser which outweighs its cost? If not, why is the purchase being considered? The buck stops with the buyer.

Self Check

---

1. How well do you buy?
2. Do you know what you want to buy before you attempt to buy it?
3. Have you specified what you want clearly?
4. Do you know your buying criteria?
5. Do you specify the buying process?
6. Do you identify the main alternative suppliers?
7. Can you work with salespeople on an even footing?
8. Can you get them to work with you rather than for you?

2.10 Sell well

Salespeople serve buyers sensitively

Every successful executive knows how to sell, even without the 'salesperson' label, and any executive can learn to sell. You sell to clients and customers who could use your organization's services, to bosses and colleagues who could back your ideas, and to suppliers whose support you might want.

Good salespeople sell people what they want to buy, whether or not they yet know it. This doesn't mean simply introducing a service and hoping someone will say, 'Where do I sign?' That virtually never happens. So how is it done?

First, you need to understand what people might want to buy. Some people will never buy what you might want to sell them. You need to know this before you waste scarce time going into a dead-end. I once came across a book called *How to sell anything to anybody*. It worked in as much as I bought the book and enjoyed the read, but no one can always sell anything to anybody. 'Sell at all costs' doesn't work in the long run and seldom works in the short run either. Most buyers can see someone who wants to sell, whether it's right for them or not, a mile off, and they put up the shutters.

Three good questions to help to understand a prospective

45

purchaser's requirements are: What's their purpose? What's their agenda? What do they really need? Until you know the answers to these questions, you aren't in a position to sell anything, except by chance.

When you understand what the buyer really wants, you are in a position to assess whether what you have is likely to help. Maybe it won't, in which case you can cut short your attempts to sell. You may earn trust with the prospective purchaser by doing so, and that trust may be helpful in future. Maybe what you have won't be helpful today but could be helpful in future, in which case you might agree to bring your communication to a close now, and review the status at a future date. Or it could be that you can see how what you have to offer could be helpful. If so, you proceed.

It's a good idea at this point to check that you really do understand the other party's requirement. You will have been listening closely, so you should now be able to state the prospective purchaser's requirement clearly and concisely. Once you have done so, ask whether you have understood correctly. Maybe something has been omitted from the exchange.

You might think that now is the moment you reveal what it is you have to sell. No, you don't! Instead you focus on the benefits of what it is you have to sell. You need to describe each of the benefits and see whether they really are benefits as far as the prospective purchaser is concerned. So, ask a question about each of them, otherwise you may never know what are benefits to this particular person. Asking is simple. The questions may be preceded by a brief statement: 'Our such-and-such service can do this, can you see that being helpful to you?' and so on, varying your turns of phrase. There's no magic to this, you are simply finding out what the other party actually appreciates. Depending upon the responses given, you are going to have a pretty good idea of how helpful the service will be and why. You are now in a position to convince your prospect to make a purchase.

Once this interchange is complete, you may want to describe the service briefly in terms of its benefits, emphasizing those that are relevant and finishing with a question like, 'Can you envisage this service being helpful to you?' You must stop talking after you ask this question – an injunction that applies similarly to every other question you ask – and wait for the answer. The prospective purchaser is beginning to make a decision. He or she is envisaging the idea working, the service being applied, the product in use, or whatever it is. While they are thinking and you are being quiet, you should be watching their body language in order to anticipate the reply.

If the prospective purchaser starts leaning towards you, they are probably about to say something positive. Let the positive reply happen. If he or she looks away and moves away from you, you may expect a negative reply is being formed. Watch out for the negative reply. You may want to jump in just before it would have been said, with a brief statement along the lines of: 'You are clearly thinking about this carefully, can I just check I understand how the service will work for you?' and go over the key benefits, before asking again whether the other party can see the service being helpful.

In this example, I have used the words 'see' and 'envisaged'. In practice, some people use a visually-oriented vocabulary, some an audio-oriented vocabulary (phrases like 'I hear you' and 'I like the sound of that'), and some use a physical-oriented vocabulary ('that feels OK'). Anyway, the best salespeople use the language that the person they are with prefers to use themselves. So listen carefully and let your words reflect the language with which the prospective buyer is most comfortable.

If the prospective buyer doesn't envisage using the service, there's a problem. Perhaps you have misread the other person's understanding. Perhaps they have misunderstood the benefits. There may well be a specific but as yet undisclosed problem. It could be anything. Whatever it is, you need to find out. You won't do anything which is likely to confirm an outright refusal until and unless you are convinced that a sale should not be made to this particular person. You may ask a series of questions which are designed to illuminate any areas about which the prospective purchaser has doubts. As soon as you find one, you want to make sufficient time to ensure you really understand the prospective purchaser's point of view. If you can't get at it by asking about specific areas, you may just have to ask: 'What would need to change for you to feel keen about using the service?' With any luck the buyer will now confess the objection, and you may be able to deal with it.

Salespeople succeed by listening, and they make sure they listen to the right things by asking most of the questions. They get buyers to do most of the talking. You could talk your way through almost all of the time that may be allotted for a meeting before you find out what really interests the buyer. If you don't understand their criteria, you don't know what you are dealing with. In fact, another way to approach a sales meeting is to ask the prospective purchaser what criteria you must meet in order for him or her to recommend a purchase be made. This last clause nullifies the objection that, 'I can't say, I would have to ask my colleagues'.

Once someone has told you their criteria, and you know what your service can do, you know whether or not a sale can be made. You may be able to say truthfully, 'So if I can show you that our service meets those criteria, will you recommend a purchase?' and wait for the reply. You can tailor everything that you know about your service to meeting those criteria. If you conclude that your service can do so, you are probably on to other perhaps unmentioned issues like the level of trust between you and the person you with whom you are dealing. And the best way to build that trust is by being as sensitive and as open as possible.

One way to help you to sell is to imagine the sale being made. That's self-envisioning. Another is to get the buyer to imagine the sale being made. You can do this by getting the buyer to think through how things would work if the sale really had been made. You may be able to say, 'Can we look at how this would work in practice. We would do this . . . You will do that . . . is that how you see it working?' and so on. Or even simply, 'How do you see yourself using the service?'

You do want to know about any objections the prospective customer may have, but you don't have to take them all on directly and you certainly don't want to argue. Instead, you may be able to go straight past them and simply focus on how things would work.

If you think a service is right for someone and you think they realize it's good too, you may be able to 'close the sale'. You may be able to ask a question the answer to which confirms that the purchaser will make a purchase, while also sorting some of the detail as well. For example, 'When do you want the service to be available?' Of course, if you have misread things, you might be given the answer, 'I don't!' But if you have got it right, the response may be 'Thursday', and a sale is becoming more certain. Alternatively you might say, 'Will Friday be soon enough to deliver the service?' At this point the prospective customer is thinking about exactly when they need the service. Whether they answer, 'Yes, that's fine,' or 'Could it be ready sooner than that?' you are probably OK. If you keep getting acceptable responses, you can keep moving until everything is sorted.

Once it is, you might just run over what you think has been agreed, for example, 'So, we will make the service available from Tuesday morning on our standard terms'.

Self Check

1. How much of your time are you selling something?
2. Do you know what you are selling?
3. Do you understand the prospective buyer's purposes?
4. Do you understand their immediate agenda?
5. Do you understand their needs?
6. Can you envisage how your service would fit in?
7. Why should the prospective buyer want to buy it?
8. Can you describe the service's features?
9. Can you express the service's benefits?
10. Can you see which benefits apply in each situation?
11. Can you ask a prospective buyer if they will make a purchase?
12. How do you sell?

2.11 Negotiate not no-gotiate

Successful executives sort the fat from the lean

How high can you jump if I lift you as you leap? And maybe you could help me soar. Some people think negotiation is a trial of strength: 'It's me against the other side,' they might say. 'We need to be tougher than them. We are going to win!' This overlooks several facts. First, there need be no conflict at all. We want to do well, they want to do well, and if we can't both do well, we should probably be somewhere else. Second, the person we are negotiating with may become or may already be a colleague, customer, or supplier, all of which relationships require trust to be effective, so we want to work with them, not against them. Third, by working together we may come up with a solution that is better than either party had in mind. So, successful negotiators use both parties' strength to work for the benefit of both parties, not to set one against the other.

Even if the macho, me-against-the-world negotiator ever manages to conclude a deal, it will probably fall apart afterwards because it is not in both parties' interest, contract or no contract; and in the meantime the ill will of an unbalanced agreement will make things difficult.

You are looking for innovative solutions. You'll remember that: Jack Sprat could eat no fat, his wife could eat no lean and so *between them both* – you remembered? – they licked the platter clean.

You might think that the other party wants this, that and the other – but if you make the time to ask, 'Why do you want this?' 'Why do you want that?' and so on, you might find that they don't, or they don't want it much. Or you could provide it in another format. Or you might discover that it's really important to them and you could give them even more of it, so making the whole deal worth much more to them.

Effective negotiation is a high-level skill which can work to both parties' benefit. Bad negotiators frustrate their own side just as much as they frustrate the other side because they block good deals. Good negotiators want to negotiate not no-gotiate.

A successful negotiator will try to maximize the value of the deal to the other party. Why? Because then they will want it all the more. They will be keener on the deal and willing to pay more. So you should try to find out what they want, and when it looks as though it is understood, try to find other things that they might want, and see if they could be fitted in too. A negotiation can be an effective sales tool.

If you start by trying to understand what the other side wants out of the deal, you'll be in a much better position to see whether you can deliver. Also, if you listen hard to them, they are more likely to listen to your requests. The last thing a good negotiator will try to do is beat the other side over the head.

And the second last thing to do is bring in the lawyers. It may be helpful to have a bit of advice from your lawyers, while you are still looking at the principles, but my experience is that the lawyers don't invent the business context, they simply respond to it. So work out your principles first. If at all possible, reach agreement. If you can't reach agreement without lawyers present, your chances of doing so quickly with lawyers present are miniscule.

It may seem obvious that a good deal is one which benefits both parties, and you may think that a deal which wouldn't benefit both parties should not be concluded, but both parties often try to pursue their own interest at the expense of the other. It isn't always the lawyers' fault. (By the way, there are some very good commercial lawyers around. The problem may lie with what they think their clients want from them, or even with what they actually want from them.) Some negotiations go round in circles and others grind to a halt. Still others stagger on for long periods of time – both sides wanting to stay busy, and perhaps enjoying the process – before a sub-optimal outcome is achieved. Neither party really understood the other nor felt good about the other or the deal, so compromise was all that was achieved. Or just two legal bills.

The key to effective negotiation is for those involved to try to find a deal that will benefit both parties. Once it's been identified, a 'win–win' deal is more likely to be concluded than a 'win–lose' or a 'lose–win' deal. It isn't simply a matter of carving up the cake since the cake doesn't have to stay the same size. You can bake a bigger cake.

A win–win deal in which both parties do well is much more likely to be followed up by another deal because both parties still feel good about it even after the ink is dry. Win–lose deals are bad for long-term business. Losers don't like to lose again.

Thinking win–win gets both parties round to the same side of the table. We are both trying to win for each other as well as ourselves. We would work for one another if we were colleagues, wouldn't we? So why wouldn't we work for one another when we are in different but potentially collaborative companies? What has changed? Are we suddenly to think ill of one another because we don't work in the same company? Is tribalism still alive and well in some quarters?

Thinking the win–win way allows the possibility of new formulations being found through working together. We are using our energies to work on the solution instead of using them to fight each other.

What if we can't reach terms that suit both sides? Maybe the time wasn't right. Maybe the deal couldn't be right. Maybe some of the people weren't right. We can walk away and leave the door open to come back another time. If you can't reach a win–win agreement it may be better to go for no deal, and bake a new cake or invent a pie.

Don't get committed to a deal until you have a deal that you can get committed to.

Self Check

1. Do you know what outcome you want to achieve?
2. Are you committed to both parties doing well?
3. Do you understand what the other party could bring to the deal?
4. Do you understand what the other party could get out of the deal?
5. Do you know what outcome they want to achieve?
6. Are you willing to work with them to realize both outcomes?
7. Can you check that you both understand all of the possible benefits?
8. Are you committed to trying to achieve them?

2.12 Delegate precisely

Successful executives park work precisely

Successful executives constantly work as part of a team. They may be in several teams at once and they may overlap. Team members constantly delegate to one another, but what is it they delegate?

Most team tasks fail because of imprecise delegation or, worse still, no delegation at all. The task itself is poorly or incompletely explained; or if well explained is given orally only and isn't completely recorded or absorbed by its recipient; or it is a well-written brief but it wasn't signed off by the writer's manager and isn't quite what he has in mind; maybe it's a good, well-written and signed-off brief but it's issued too late for work of sufficient quality to be done; or the brief is given to the wrong executive or team. Perhaps, even more commonly, the task was never delegated at all. It was hung on to by someone who didn't find the time to do it. They felt pressured, valued, even heroic, but they died with the ball.

Even junior executives have opportunities to delegate, to assistants, receptionists, secretaries, and others too – most of all, to one another. 'I need some help. Can you find me a few minutes today so I can tell you what I need?' may seem easy enough to say, but it means admitting you aren't superhuman, and no executive is. A key difference is that successful executives know they must rely on others to succeed, and have come to terms with this knowledge.

To delegate you need to identify something that you don't have, and someone with the skills to create it. When you delegate, describe the thing you want created, for example what needs to be delivered to whom and when.

For instance, 'I would like your help. We need to provide a report by this time tomorrow. One part of the report concerns the significant trends. They are somewhere in these printouts. Can you review them and identify the important trends and provide a report on disk by 9.30 am so I can write the report on time?' You may not need to describe how it should be done. Working out how best to do it may be a key part of the task you are delegating, and the person you are delegating to may already have a better idea of how to do it. You may not want to impose your methods.

Think about the work that you do very well. How much of it could be done better by someone else? How much could you delegate to someone else? If you gave that to them you would be free yourself to take on other work. Maybe that work would be more enjoyable. Maybe you could add more value by doing it.

You shouldn't try to delegate work just because you don't enjoy it or because you're not very good at it. You should delegate work once you have become very good at it, so good that you can show someone else. Then they can become good too.

Self Check

1. Who can help you do your work?
2. Who can help you to be more effective?
3. What can each of them do?
4. What does each person need to know in order to do the task?
5. When would you need each of the tasks completed?
6. What guidance to the quality of the work is needed?
7. Do you check that the work is done OK?
8. Do you give appropriate feedback?
9. How much of your work could someone else do as well as you?
10. Could you delegate that to them and get into more interesting work?

Chapter Three

Work Well in Time

Imagine you are on an old film set. A single camera provides the sole view of events. It has one fixed focus which is looking twelve feet ahead. Everything nearer or further away than twelve feet is fuzzy.

Most of us spend most of our working lives looking about twelve feet ahead. Or twelve minutes. We don't see what is happening right now too clearly, nor do we see things further out, we just see the next few minutes. Successful executives can adjust their focus, they can concentrate on the here and now. They can also look twelve days, weeks or months out. When things look fuzzy to them, they adjust the lens.

3.1 Manage projects in good time

Successful executives project forward

You may be asked to manage a project. How should you go about it? Start by specifying the final result. Get that clear in your own mind. What is it that needs to be produced? What would a good outcome look like? Who would have to be satisfied with it? What are they looking for? How will your work be tested after you have completed it? How robust does it need to be?

Then you can get on to the specifics. Exactly what needs to be delivered to whom and when? What are the various elements of the project? What do these elements need before they can even be started? In what order do they need to be produced?

Then there is the final delivery date. Can you deliver on time? What's most likely to give? How would you find alternative sources if necessary? How big a problem is it if you miss the final delivery time? Are you likely to need more time? Can you get more time? How much room for manoeuvre do you need? You should aim to work within the deadlines and give yourself some slack; you may need it.

You'll need to make a list of the resources you require, and what about the people? Can you select them, will someone else select them, or have they already been assigned? How much of their time are you likely to need? How much of their time has been allocated? Can you get any more?

You will need to communicate clearly with each member of the team who reports to you. How do they see their part of the task? What will their work look like when it comes to you? Do they have in mind what you have in mind? If not, is what they have in mind as good or better? Have they considered how they will go about their task? Will that work? Do they understand the deadline?

How will reportees tell you of their progress? How quickly do they need to let you know of anything which is likely to make them late? Will it help them to know of others' progress? How often does the team need to meet? How will you keep them motivated and hold them accountable?

You want to know what's going on as the project develops. Sometimes you'll have to contain your desire to know, just to ensure you respect people's space, but sometimes you will need to know. Every time you ask them, you reduce their obligation to volunteer news in future. You want your team to tell you the truth, but they will only bring you the truth if they think it won't scare you. So you'll need to keep calm if and when things go wrong, or you won't hear about the next crisis until even later! Attack the messenger, and you may not get any more messages.

You may not want to take ownership of the crisis away from them. After all, a crisis is a learning opportunity. You may want to show them how they can sort it out. You can take them through a process of looking at the crisis until they can identify alternative courses of action. Then you will evaluate them. But you might help them the most if you simply continue to affirm your faith in their ability to solve the problem.

Your team could learn that you will support them even in a crisis. (Or they could learn that you lose your nerve even more easily than they do.)

Self Check

1. What are the items that need to be delivered?
2. In what sequence do they need to be created?
3. Exactly when do they need to be delivered?
4. Who is best placed to deliver each of them?
5. What other resources are required?
6. When do they need to be briefed?
7. What information needs to go in each brief?
8. How will you manage the project?
9. What information does each person need as the project develops?
10. How will you handle crises?

3.2 Give value

Successful executives give the extra smile

Everybody loves a giver. Usually, you have to give before you can get. Taking without giving is a one-way trade and is difficult to pull off. In the natural world, you can't reap what you haven't sown, your crop won't grow until you plant it. Similar principles seem to apply in business. Anyway, giving value is a practical policy. Wherever you are, whatever you are doing, you can always give, but you can't always take. So giving is easier than getting! It comes first.

And the more you give, the more you are likely to get. That doesn't mean giving aimlessly, thoughtlessly or foolishly; but give and a reward will be yours, although perhaps not immediately, or from where you expected. It may seem to you that you have failed, that you have given and absolutely nothing has come back, but failure often precedes success, if only you will keep on going.

The return may not be in a form you anticipated. Or may not be from the source you expected. My experience is that when I've worked flat out to bring in business, it has come, but not always where I thought it would come from, and not always when I thought it was needed. I couldn't see what was happening behind the scenes. I couldn't see what I was planting where. But the business was out there, all the same, and it materialized.

Whenever you can, give more than has been asked. That wouldn't necessarily mean a longer report, it would mean a better one. The difference between underperformance and superperformance can be small in terms of effort, but the results may be very different. Go the extra mile.

Every time you give gladly and willingly you are likely to strengthen a relationship with someone, whom you may need in future. You are showing them that you are willing to work with them, that you aren't on another side, that they can trust you to deliver. Get yourself into a virtuous circle. Give the extra smile.

Self Check

1. Do you start out by trying to give?
2. Or is your initial emphasis on what you can get?
3. Do you try to provide more than was asked for?
4. Are you willing to go the extra mile?
5. Do you provide service with a smile?

3.3 Never attack people

See others' strengths and your weaknesses

Brace yourself! Quick! Duck! 'You'll never succeed.' 'You'll never manage to do that.' 'What did I tell you?' You don't have to accept or reject negative or destructive comments from other people. Their scripts can remain their scripts if you don't accept or reject them. You can sidestep them one and all.

You don't have to take them personally or use your energy fighting them. You can simply decline to engage them. You can watch them go by. You can allow them to remain the property of the person who has proffered them.

From your point of view, you might think someone is talking baloney. You don't have to say it and you don't have to be quiet either. Instead, try listening closely to what's being said and feed it back to the other person in your own words and without bias, for instance: 'Let me see if I understand what you are saying, you think . . .' Be fair in your interpretation. This gives the other person a chance to hear what it is they have said. They may not have paid attention to their own words until now. You will quite often find they then want to express themselves rather differently. You have helped to straighten things out without creating conflict.

Destructive ideas have a power of their own. They tend to squeeze out a constructive frame of mind and discourage construction. They are as unwelcome as the destruction they precede. Constructive thoughts precede constructive action. The same applies to negative thoughts. What's good about thinking negatively? Nothing, unless you want nothing to happen. Be a builder, not a pillager.

There are a lot of things that effective executives don't do. They never assume things. When something wasn't done, or was done wrongly and you ask the person involved what happened, do you sometimes hear a response that begins 'I assumed that . . .' In other words, they didn't check. When we don't check something out, we often wish we had done so. You can check things out.

Don't turn a guess into a categorical statement. 'Maybe', 'perhaps' and 'could' are handy business words that can truthfully reflect our knowledge and prevent backtracking. A guess is a guess, an estimate is an estimate, an opinion is just an opinion. Nothing more. You are free to use your judgement to act on the basis that anything may or may not be true. You can take responsibility for your judgement.

Own up when you make a mistake and someone wants to

know what happened. I once made a purchase without a client's authority and thought he would be pleased. He wasn't. He called demanding to know how it had happened. I jumped in. 'I booked it. I did it.' His aggression evaporated. Cover-ups multiply many problems. Their discovery upsets people and cuts down trust. You can prevent a disaster from snowballing. It's called damage limitation.

And don't criticize others. Of course, we all make mistakes, none of us is perfect, and all of us can change and improve. The next time you hear a cutting criticism, imagine that the criticism is being made of that person. Quite often, the cap fits. To say that 'Criticism is for the kids' would be unfair on the kids. Just leave it out!

Self Check

1. Do you think positively?
2. How do you handle negative thoughts?
3. Do you allow them to disturb your concentration?
4. Can you let them walk on by?
5. Do you ever say 'I assumed . . .' when something has gone wrong?
6. Do you tend to check things thoroughly?
7. Do you represent a guess as though it were true?

3.4 Organize your time

Know your schedule

Why organize your time? Not everybody does. Why not just let the work come to you, and deal with the needs of the moment? There's more than enough to do, anyway, isn't organizing time dull?

Time is your only resource. It's the one thing which is constantly disappearing. Make better use of it and you increase your productivity. You can work flat out but achieve very little if you don't use your time well. You may be working on the wrong things or neglecting key tasks.

Just getting up, having breakfast and getting to the office can seem more than enough effort for one day, especially if you are not in good shape. And then there's all those chores to be done when you get to work. Completing all the tasks that other people throw at you can de-motivate you, and being stopped from completing the tasks you start can be even worse. There is a way through this problem.

To manage time well you must understand your **P**riorities, **O**rganise to achieve them, **E**xecute the necessary tasks, and **T**hink about what you've achieved and should achieve next, and **R**echarge **Y**ourself. Try to memorize 'POETRY'!

Some things are more important than others. You need to make a priority of the important things, but you can't do that unless you have worked out what they are. If you are usually busy, you can only find time for the important things if you slot them into your schedule before it gets full with urgent work. Your priorities will change from week to week, so you need to review them regularly to check they reflect what you really want to achieve next. The following sections show you how you can achieve more in limited time.

Self Check

1. Do you want to be in charge of your schedule?
2. Or would you prefer that someone else was?
3. Or perhaps that you didn't have a schedule at all?
4. Can you create a schedule and master it?

3.5 Set up your day every day

Manage your days before they disappear

Start by organizing each day in advance. Before you begin, preferably before you meet your colleagues, make a list of all the things you want to get done that day. Group the tasks by project and estimate roughly how many minutes of your time each task is likely to take. I usually pencil in 15", 30", 60" or 120" beside each thing I want to do. You may be looking, for example, at 400 minutes of tasks. You may also want to make a list of business or domestic tasks you want to get done on the way home, or when you get home. They're important too.

To start off, you may have no idea how long each task will take. You may not even know how you currently spend your time. As you make each day's list and review yesterday's list you will quickly see how you spend your time and get better at estimating how long things will take. Sometimes I revise my time estimates as I go through the day. If something took me 30 minutes not the expected 15 minutes, I can change the time estimate right away, and make a better estimate next time.

Now you know what you need to achieve. Cross off each task as you complete it. This can be very satisfying. You'll know when you had a successful day because you'll see that you got everything done. If at any point during the day you aren't sure what to do next, refer to the list and move straight on to the next task. It saves time wondering fruitlessly. Add tasks to the list as new jobs come your way. Your action list will help you to defend yourself against taking on too much or agreeing to do things sooner than you'll be able to manage.

At what time of day are you at your most effective? Many of us peak in the morning, dip after lunch and get to a higher level of performance later in the afternoon. I seem to be at my most cogent before 9 in the morning and after 8 at night, so that's when I do most of my thinking. (You don't need to be at an office to think; in fact, thinking in an open plan office can be difficult.) The rest of the day is execution, development and recreation. Plan your important work around your peaks.

Your goal may be to do all the work you plan to get done today. Why don't you go home when it's done? By all means think about tomorrow on your way home. Some executive cultures may seem to require you to work all hours. Such a culture is counter-productive, resulting in people hanging around underachieving while staying chained to the desk. I visited such an office and found the time was filled with work-related banter and inconclusive discussion. I wanted to ask them: 'How are you being paid?' which might have perplexed them, and then follow up with: 'You mean you get money just for talking with one another?' but it wasn't my place to ask these questions. I bit my tongue.

While it's sometimes necessary to put in extra hours there's no merit in putting in time for its own sake. You should be paid to produce, not to fill in the time. Before long, you should be able to show your manager a higher level of productivity than the desk-sitters. The beauty about focusing on results is you know when you are being effective. When I can get my work done on time, I go home. Sometimes I treat myself. If I can speed up and get my work done early, I go early, but don't leave the office unless it's OK with your boss!

If you haven't done one before, try an **ABCDEF** Daily Action list like the one below.

Minutes	Action	Complete process forms
	Be with	
90	Nick	Project review meeting
60	Tim	Progress review
15	Call	Tim re feedback. What does he think?
15		Angela re progress with sales
	Dictate	
60		Clear Request for Information
30	Edit	Proposal and issue
60	Friends	Get present for Sue

This groups tasks by type to help you focus on one kind of task at a time. The important thing is to begin each task with an idea of how you want it to finish. 'Call Jill' is not sufficient. 'Call Jill to agree next action steps' may be what you need to do.

One day's work usually begins to generate the next, and overnight reflection adds more. So you can begin work on tomorrow's list today and start with anything that is left over from today. Daily list-making is invaluable for fire-fighting, because it helps you to keep the flames at bay. Without such a list you are likely to get burnt, but to stop fires starting, you need to make weekly plans.

Self Check

1. What are the key things you achieve every day?
2. What are the tasks that crop up occasionally?
3. Where are you spending most of your time?
4. How much of your activity is productive?
5. Where are you getting most of your results?
6. Do you identify your priorities before you begin your day?
7. Are you more effective when you do so?
8. At what times of day are you most effective?

3.6 Set the lunch

Lunch can be an outstanding investment

People are important. A business breakfast, lunch or dinner is an opportunity to show someone they are special. It's also a great opportunity to listen because you can learn so much more about a person over lunch than in an office meeting.

It can be a very effective way to help to build a relationship. The lunch can have significance, even without a particular agenda, simply because you sit down together in one another's company without the constraints of the office. (Incidentally, if you want a routine meeting to be more productive than usual – perhaps it has got into a rut – try moving it somewhere else, like a hotel. Participants are likely to behave differently.) You may have some ideas you want to put forward to a client, manager or peer. You could call the other person and ask if it would be OK if you discussed these over lunch.

That gives your ideas legitimacy when you get around to considering them.

You don't need to wait for the invitations to pour in because you can issue some yourself. A business lunch can be a remarkably good investment, even if you have to meet the bill. Inviting someone to lunch is an art in itself. It's generally better to ask the person you are inviting which would be a good week and then, if that week is good, the best day. Following up an oral agreement with a written note confirming the details avoids any possible misunderstanding.

You now have an opportunity to get to know the person you are with rather better. In an office meeting it is seldom appropriate to enquire about someone's personal circumstances, but during a business lunch you normally can do so.

You can also show interest in, and seek to understand, someone's overall objectives in their job, and at their company. Also, you may be able to get a better understanding of how much or how little they appreciate aspects of any services you provide. They may also be able to show you ways you could provide more value. All of this can help you to work more effectively with that person.

The lunch doesn't have to last all afternoon. The second half hour may provide most of the value. You can maximize the value of what you hear and understand by writing up the lunch afterwards. Otherwise you are likely to forget most of the detail.

If you refresh your memory by looking at your file note on the lunch before your next meeting, even before any following lunch, you are likely to find that your guest (or host) is amazed at the degree of personal attention you have given him. He will feel special.

You can follow up the lunch at the appropriate time in a tone that's consistent with the lunch itself. Go over what happened at the lunch and think about useful things that you can do before you call or write; you can then build on the relationship naturally. If you were the guest at the lunch, you absolutely must follow up with a letter of thanks within a day or two. It's amazing how many people don't, so you actually get ahead every time you do.

Self Check

---

1. Who do you need to spend time with?
2. How do you prepare for a business lunch?
3. Do you make a list of the subjects you want to explore?
4. Do you make a note after the lunch and place it on file?
5. How do you follow up the lunch?
6. Which other relationships could you improve?

3.7 At the end of the day

Time is the one thing you can't re-create

One of the keys to organization is to organize yourself before you take action, and the best time to get organized for today was yesterday. Bad luck! But the best time to review today is towards the end of it, and it's also the best time to get organized for tomorrow.

Use the end of the day to review your progress while events are still fresh in your mind. Do it before you leave the office, on the train, or even at home, whenever works best for you. Make some time to see what you have accomplished and what remains to be done. How did you do? What's still left on today's list? How are you doing with the important tasks you set yourself at the beginning of the week?

Make sure incomplete tasks go on to tomorrow's daily list. Also look at where you spent your time. Time is your most valuable commodity. Use it up and you've nothing left. If you have to complete a company time sheet, do so at the end of the day. If you aren't expected to do so, use your action list to see where you spent your time. What did you get done? How long did it take? Did you manage to spend your time working on achieving your priorities? Or did you move off target?

Be honest with yourself. Look at what you didn't do. Is that a problem? Look at what you achieved. What was your time budget for the tasks that you completed? More or less than a day's work? What else did you get done?

How could you have done better and where did you go wrong? If you didn't get a number of things done, was it because an unforeseeable crisis cropped up? If so, wouldn't it be worth thinking about what you could do to help stop such a crisis recurring?

Did you put too much on your plate to start with? In which case you need to be more realistic about what you can achieve in one day. Or did you just lose interest during the day? Ask yourself why was that? Were the goals you set yourself insufficiently motivating?

Perhaps you got everything done and then some. That's when you strengthen yourself. Maybe you could aim a bit higher tomorrow, but not so high that you invite failure.

The really good thing is that you can learn from today and do better tomorrow. Get 1 per cent better at your work every day, and you will be twice as effective in a few months!

Self Check

1. How effective are you at the end of the day?
2. Have you noticed how effective you were yesterday?
3. Where did you spend your time?
4. Did you manage to stay focused on your priorities?
5. Or did you get deflected on to other things?
6. Have you looked at what worked and what didn't?
7. Have you thought about which things you should do differently?
8. Have you begun to prepare for tomorrow?
9. Have you tried taking some quiet time early in the morning?
10. What effect did that have on your day?

3.8 Throughout the week

Weekly planning moves you up a gear

Daily list-making and execution is a vital but incomplete basis for organization. On its own, it tends to produce a strong bias towards completing urgent activities, towards doing what other people ask you to do. That's fine as far as it goes because you can't help but do the urgent stuff.

However, without longer term planning, less urgent but often no less important activities will tend to be neglected. If there's a strong bias towards daily planning, some non-urgent but important work may never be done – like investing in people, processes and your own ability. And if you don't improve those, you won't improve much.

You will get a slightly longer term perspective by planning the week. To get the best results, you need to do rather more than when you plan the day. A simple list won't do. To begin to set your own agenda, think about your different roles as an executive and also in your non-executive life.

You may work on a number of projects, or for a number of bosses. Then there's your social life too. If you haven't done so, make a list of the five to seven most important roles you fulfil. Try looking at the two or three most important parts of your executive life. You also have a role within your family or home. Maybe you are active in a voluntary group of some kind or you pursue a fulfilling hobby or interest. That's important too. And remember to include your own self-development as one of the most central roles.

For each of these roles, try to identify a single thing you could do that would make a big contribution this week. Take time to do this and see what comes up for you. Everyone's list is different, and changes each week. Your list may include tasks that will take you time in the short run but will save you lots of time in the long run. If you've been fire-fighting for months, or even years, your important list may include things that have been coming into your mind for an awfully long time. It may seem to you that there's never been enough time, yet only by doing them will you find more time.

You may think you can't find the time for these things. Well, how much time have you spent sitting in front of a TV or video screen in the past week? Two hours? Six hours? More? And how much time did you spend idly chatting without a purpose in mind? If you found time for such unproductive activities, couldn't you find time to do the things that are important to you?

Think about the coming week. What would be the right amount of time to spend watching TV? No time? One hour? More? You can free up a lot of time without denying yourself every pleasure. I am not saying you shouldn't have any time for leisure. Rest is important and I still spend some time self-indulgently, but only for a few hours a week. It's under my control.

Don't be tempted to select too many important things in your schedule in any one week. One or at most two per role seems sufficient. *Doing* the tasks you commit yourself to is important, and achieving, or even over-achieving, gets you into a virtuous circle.

You should set about achieving the important things. Quite possibly, none of them was on your daily list because none of them was urgent, but all of them are important to you. Now your challenge is to fit these important things into your week before they get crowded out by the urgent daily things that usually eat up your time. Let the daily tasks fit around the weekly priorities you have identified and use your will to get to the weekly priorities.

Reviewing your progress against your key goals mid-week and at the end of the week is crucial. You need to know if you are achieving the weekly goals you have set yourself. No one else needs to know, but you do. You may start by scoring two or three out of about seven tasks. Well, that's a start. That may be two or three more important (non-urgent) tasks completed than in the previous week and some of them may save you time in the coming weeks, enabling you to get more such work done. Next week, you might get up to four out of seven such tasks completed, and so on.

Use the end of the week, or the weekend, to review your success in achieving last week's goals. Look at any you haven't achieved. Should you make a point of achieving them in the coming week, should you pencil them in a week or two out, or drop them from your goals entirely? Now you can begin to plan next week's goals. The ones that will really make a difference.

Self Check

1. Are you locked into day to day urgent actions?
2. Do you get around to important but non-urgent work?
3. Do you plan your week in advance?
4. Do you identify the outcomes you want?
5. Do you know in advance what would represent a successful week?
6. Are you working to a weekly plan?
7. Are you working to any plan of your own?
8. How much time do you want to spend on self-indulgence?
9. Do you check at the end of the week to see how you did?
10. Do you set fresh goals for the coming week?

3.9 Throughout the month

Monthly planning is more powerful still

If you have been planning your days, or haven't been planning at all, you may find moving to weekly planning a big enough leap to make in one go. If you haven't done so, try weekly planning now.

Once you have mastered weekly planning, or even sooner, try planning the month. Planning the month gives you even more leverage. It may be obvious that you can accomplish more in a month than in a week. It may not be so obvious that you can accomplish more in a month than you can in four and a bit separate weeks. To do so, treat the month as a whole.

At the end of this month, take some time to reflect on what you want to achieve next month. What are the important

71

priorities for you? The answers may not spring forward. You may need to allow some time. Most things that come to mind will be things that you need to act upon. You need to take the initiative.

What do you want to achieve in your work? What do you want to do at home? It may be something that's been bugging you for months. What do you want to do for or with each of the people who are important to you? What new skill do you want to acquire? Perhaps something that's going to enable you to do one or two things just a little bit better? Or something that will make your world a slightly better place.

You may want to include a set of financial goals, especially if your income moves directly in line with some other numbers. Even if it doesn't, you may find it helpful to include the most relevant monthly number in your monthly plan. You can include even bigger goals in monthly planning because you have more time in which to achieve them. Each monthly plan will begin to provide a context for your weekly plan. In some roles, the weekly plans will become stepping stones on the way to achieving your annual plan!

Apart from the things that are thrown at you every day, something else is happening. Instead of being at the mercy of daily events, you impose a well-thought-out agenda of your own. Your weekly goals begin to emerge from your monthly goals, and form part of a bigger context.

You may want to think about your role as part of a family too. How could you make a powerful contribution to its well-being next month?

For instance, when it comes to self-development you may well find it better to focus on one set of skills in each month and then go after aspects of them each week. You may want to focus on time management skills this month, get into some PC training next month and then practise your presentation skills in the following month. Achieving and maintaining excellence is a never-ending process.

Self Check

> 1. Do you plan your month in advance?
> 2. What could you achieve next month?
> 3. What are your targets for the month?
> 4. Do you keep a note of how you spend your time each month?
> 5. How much of your time do you spend working on your monthly goals?

3.10 Throughout the year

You could make this year the best one to date

Most executives live out other people's agendas. They may look for their own ways to do things each day, week and month, but in the longer term, they are working within the constraints of other people's purposes. Creating and controlling your own agenda isn't easy, but you will increase your control if you get clear on your own medium- and long-term objectives.

Annual planning can be a powerful weapon in your armoury. A year provides a good period of time to frame some of your lifetime objectives. They can be big objectives which may motivate you more. You may want to have a salary or income increase. If you do, it's important to support this with ways of providing extra value to your firm, or at least a commitment to do so. Years ago, I would link being 'brilliant' at my work with earning a particular annual percentage rise in my salary. It worked. The principle is to deliver more value to receive more value.

You don't have to wait until December to start to frame next year's plans, you can start now, and begin the year as soon as you are clear on your objectives.

If you don't currently have any objectives for this year, start with a blank sheet of paper and try to answer some of the questions below. You may have objectives for your work, your own skills base and your income, as well as your home and your family. Don't be afraid to be ambitious. How

73

do you know what you could achieve until you try? What are your limits? Have you reached any yet?

If you already have some objectives, are you on target to achieve them? If not, what new action could you take to help you to get there?

If you set objectives for last year and you achieved them, you have a powerful platform on which to build and achieve new objectives this year. Building each year's goals on top of those of the previous one can powerfully direct your career onward.

The successful executive takes holidays too. He knows that they are crucial to re-creation. Without them you are likely to get more and more stale, maybe without even noticing. If you don't take breaks and are still managing, just think how much more powerful you could be after a break or two.

Self Check

1. Where do you want to be in a year's time?
2. What kind of projects would you like to be working on?
3. What sort of solutions would you like to be coming up with?
4. What new skills would you like to be exercising?
5. What salary do you think you should be earning?
6. How could you provide more value to your firm?
7. How could you help it to provide more value to its customers?
8. How could you help your boss do a better job without getting yourself out of line?
9. What do you want to achieve or contribute outside your work?

3.11 Inspired by a mission

Your long-term purpose can give you purpose every day

Even a year is only a small part of a typical executive's career.

To get into the highest and most powerful form of planning, you need to look at your executive career, even your life, as a whole, not just a little bit of it.

Look back over your career to date. Have there been periods when you have been successful, and other periods when you have been unsuccessful? What was different about those times? What was different about the circumstances? What did you do differently? What have you learnt from that?

Many people are doing what they are doing because that's the way it just happened. They are living where they are living through force of circumstance too. Instead of making it happen, life has been happening to them. But what would you want to make happen? If you were in charge, what would you want to achieve?

Most very successful people have some idea of what they want. They know what their life is about. It may be partly about providing value and earning money; it may be about being the best at your work; it may be about giving service to others. It may be about all three. It can be unique to you.

You may be clear about the purpose of your own life. If you haven't yet discovered it, you may not want to make the effort that is necessary to get some clarity. You may be happier bobbing along. Yet no one else can do this work for you. If *you* don't get clear what your life is about, who will?

Take some time out to think about what your life is about. Get a pencil and paper handy, look at the questions below and then shut your eyes.

Self Check

1. What do you want to achieve in your career?
2. What contribution do you want to make?
3. What do you really want to do with your life?
4. What sort of plans have you made to realize your goals?
5. Could you make a start on your life's work this year?
6. If not this year, when?

Did you shut your eyes? If not, do give it a whirl. What came up? How do you feel about it? Do you have any sense of a direction? If not, keep coming back to it!

3.12 Work for long-term results

The greater the depths, the greater the heights

This is the superficial age. The time of instant results. The quick-fix urge. You can hear it even in a dinner party conversation – whatever you do, don't discuss anything too deep, nothing that would affect us, nothing that would shake our comfortable security.

I once worked on a business plan in which I suggested the actions required now as part of the short-term plan, the actions required at some point in the future as part of the medium-term plan, and the long-term plan included the actions that we didn't have to get around to for quite some time. The short-term plan was mainly about patching over today's crises and the long-term was about really improving the quality of the service, which would clearly take some time. I showed the draft to a colleague who pointed out to me that the long term begins now. That is, we need to start on the short, medium and long-term work immediately. In a few months' time there would be another short-term plan, but we would be continuing with the same medium and long-term plans.

For many executives, the medium and long term are never addressed. Life is simply a series of short-term time periods, but there's a low limit to what you can achieve in the short term, while you can achieve many times as much in the long term. It's there that most big achievements are made.

Most people overestimate what they can achieve in a week and underestimate what they could achieve in a decade – though few people set out to achieve something over a decade. It may be that the focus on short-term results is stronger today than usual. The short term is important, because if you neglect it you may have some problems fast. However, if you focus exclusively on the short term, you probably won't achieve anything much.

Successful executives try to be effective in the short, medium and long term – and the medium and long term begin now, not at some never to be reached point in the future.

Many people seem to have little idea what they want to achieve in their life. The long term is a mystery in which they have no interest. Yet today's actions can positively or negatively affect the long term. They can help to set someone on a course, if they did but know it.

Try to get a sense of where you might be in five or ten years' time. What might you have achieved? What might you want to achieve? Can you see how your current activity is moving you towards those goals? If not, then maybe you don't have the right goals. Alternatively, you should change your behaviour so you are working towards achieving them.

Self Check

1. What are you planning to achieve in the short term?
2. What are you planning to achieve in the next year or so?
3. What could you achieve in the next five or ten years?
4. What could you do this year to move towards that?
5. What thought have you given to the very long term?

Chapter Four

We Communicate

4.1 Your call

The telephone is your virtual meeting place

Most executives have most of their conversations on the phone. Some of this time is spent leaving or taking messages; some involves a number of people, for instance, gathered around a speaker phone. Most of it, however, is between two people, the caller and the call-taker.

Since so much business is done by phone, it makes sense to think of each call as a mini-meeting. Convention has it that the caller can set out the purposes and dictate the agenda of the phone-meeting and make most of the running during the call. The call-maker can ask the penetrating questions and drive the call towards a conclusion, subject to the consent of the call-taker.

Get relevant papers handy before you make a call. You may want to make sure you can access relevant computer files fast too. Otherwise you are likely to get stumped when you're asked a direct question. What's more, you will seem disorganized. You may also want to prepare for an answering machine facility. If you are calling to get some information, leave the request as well as your number.

So, make a list of the points you want to cover before you make the call. You can even type in the feedback as you go along.

Don't ignore the social pleasantries. They show that you care about the other person and they do tend to deepen the personal bonds that make business more rewarding. It only takes a moment or two to ask someone how they are and listen to their reply. Open questions like 'What are you up to?' may bring forth helpful information that you hadn't anticipated. Asking how the other person sees something developing may be more valuable than getting into the specifics you have in mind. They may not be what the other person has in mind at all. The best time to get into the detail is after you have checked you are looking at the same picture.

Your voice is at its most powerful on the phone. Nothing else gets a look in, and physical gestures will go unnoticed. Your voice can set a particular tone for each call. You can convey warmth, interest and friendship immediately, when you wish.

When you receive a call, you don't need to answer every question straight away. You may not have all relevant papers handy. If you don't have them handy, but think you will need them, it's better to ask for a moment to get them, or offer to call back, than to bluff. If you promise you will get back to the caller, make a note of the questions immediately. As the call-taker, you can be open about the limit of your knowledge. The onus is on the caller to have thought things through. You may be more interested in whether the caller has done so.

Calls should have an ending. You can wrap up the call by reiterating the action point or points, and confirming both parties' agreement to them. This is more important if it's a long call and the points may not have been crystal clear to you both.

Then you replace the receiver; there is a great temptation to think that the call is over and you can move on. You may be under time pressure to do so, but this is the ideal time to invest a moment or two in reflecting on the call. Did it go well? What did you achieve? What did you mis-read? What could you have done better? Were there any awkward moments? What do you need to do now? Who do you need to tell? How can you do so efficiently? How do you need to change your schedule to fit in any extra work?

Personally, I find it effective to make all the calls I have scheduled for a particular day one after the other, just allowing a bit of time between them to make any notes on the preceding call and think about the next one. Of course, some of the outbound calls that don't reach the intended call-taker will require a return call later in the day, but still, grouping calls can release other parts of the day for telephone-free activity.

You may find it helpful to add every phone number you dial to a directory. It only takes a few seconds and will free you of the problem of needing to get a number a second time and perhaps not knowing how to do so.

You will take calls that are meant for other people too. They are a great opportunity to be effective. You can approach them unencumbered by the history of the relationship. You are simply you. When you are the caller, you can get a strong impression of an organization from the people who answer calls on behalf of others. They are not supposed to speak to you, and probably don't know who you are, but they can still sound businesslike or sloppy. So give it your best shot. 'Emma Jones' office, Colin Smith speaking,' may do fine to start with. Suppose it's someone you don't know and they ask for Emma Jones who isn't around. You can say, 'I can't reach her, but can I take a message or help you in some way?' Even though you don't know the caller, you have offered to help. It's clear to the caller that taking a message would be no trouble to you. I just love dealing with people who want to be helpful. Isn't this life too short for anything else?

Do take clear phone messages. You may save the return phone call altogether. Some people scribble a name on a slip of paper and leave it by the phone. What does that mean? You need to get the name, message, what the receiver should do about the message, and whether a call back is required. You may also need to get the phone number. If in doubt, get it. There's little more feeble than: 'Did you get the number?' 'No, I thought you had it.' It's also helpful to check when would be a good time for the call back. Finally, you need to add the time of message and your name. You can then thank the caller for calling and indicate that you will get the message to Miss Jones.

If you are the call-maker and the person you want to speak to isn't around, you may be able to complete the call just by leaving a message of what you wanted to say. If a call back is needed, be ready to say when you would be available to take the call. If you are going to call back, find out when they will be around. You may get to know the schedule of people you call regularly and even set up a particular time of the week or month for your calls. This saves missed, inconvenient and under-prepared calls. It's all part of getting on top of your schedule, rather than letting your schedule get on top of you.

Self Check

1. How effective are you on the phone?
2. Do you group your calls for the day and make them one after the other?
3. When someone's out, do you specify when you could take a return call?
4. Do you begin each call knowing what you want to achieve?
5. Do you take time to set an appropriate tone?
6. Do you give the other person room to speak?
7. Do you think carefully about what they are saying?
8. Do you know what questions to ask to get the answers you need?
9. Do you confirm the action points at the end of the call?
10. Do you put data straight on to your database?
11. Do you make a note of all the calls you receive?
12. Do you return all of your calls?
13. Do you keep a call log book?
14. Do you take clear messages for others?

4.2 **Write clearly**
Write for effect, not affect

There is no point writing something that won't be read, and there is seldom any point in an executive writing something if it doesn't cause or prevent action. Executives have to make an impact on their part of the world. One way is via the written word. An executive who can get people to read words and act upon them in the way that's intended is likely to be successful.

The pressure of business life and individuals' inevitable personal discretion means they don't even read some of what they receive, let alone act on it. To begin with, you need to write well enough to get read. Beyond that, you need to write well enough for people to be able to see what you see the way you see it. Once you have done that, getting the readers to support appropriate recommendations is a piece of cake.

Your written work needs to be more precise than oral work. Written work lacks eye contact. It doesn't shrug its shoulders. It has to stand on its own. You can't see how people respond to each thought and then slip in urgently-needed caveats. Written words can be studied carefully. They may even be believed and acted upon, without so much as a by your leave. Just like this paragraph.

How should you set about writing clearly? Think through what you want to convey, marshal your facts, identify the key points of your argument, and get it on screen clearly and concisely. Are you still using pen and paper?

Prepare yourself before you sit down at your PC or pick up your dictaphone. Work out what you want to achieve before you realize how you will achieve it. If you are not yet at the point where you can begin to write, just think about your purpose. Who are the recipients? What do you want them to think? What do you want them to do after they've read your words? What can you say that would induce them to do that?

Write to length. You can have some idea of how long the letter, memo or paper should be and you can work within those limits. Make your work as succinct as possible. In general, papers more than a page long are far less likely to be read. As Winston Churchill said to the First Lord of the Admiralty, 'Pray tell me, on one sheet of paper, the requirements of His Majesty's navy for the next twelve months.'

From time to time you may get stuck when you are composing. If you do, concentrate on the points that need to be made. If you don't know them, you probably haven't given it enough thought. You need to know what to say before you can work out the best way to say it.

Give prominence to the key actions that need to be undertaken, either by putting them right at the beginning of the communication or by highlighting them in some way.

Write for action. Avoid jargon unless it's a shorthand known to all the intended readers. Make sentences as short as possible. Once it has said what it needs to, each sentence should stop.

Try to edit your own work. Well-edited work is likely to give you better results. As you look at what you have written and the structures you have created, and as you delete redundant words and phrases – like this one – you will discover ways to communicate more clearly in fewer words. After a while, your first drafts will get better.

The more you compose different kinds of business communication, the more you have to draw from. As with so many other things, practice makes perfect. It also makes you quicker.

Pack your memoranda with recommendations. Decide what action should be the result. Make the main recommendation stand out and make all of them loud and clear. Explain why they should occur, and provide any necessary back-up to support the decision. Cut the rest. You may want to send long memoranda, with lots of interesting information which doesn't directly affect what you recommend. Don't. It probably won't be read. Worse, it will get in the way of what you do want to communicate. Add detailed attachments which support your case if necessary, but don't expect everyone to read them.

Make each of your letters self-explanatory and self-contained. Your letter may be unexpected; your reader may be thinking of other things; so, explain briefly why you are writing. In doing so, you can say why the recipient should read the letter. Perhaps someone expressed interest in something and you are following up. If so, you might begin your letter, 'You wanted to know . . .'

The end of your letter should deal with the next steps. If you want to leave it to the other person to decide to take action or not, the letter might end, 'Do let me know if you need any other information to help you make your decision.' Or maybe the recipient needs the information to make a decision and you want to confirm your interest in that, too. In which case you might add something like, 'I look forward to the outcome.' Only if you do, of course.

Status Reports can be powerful business tools. Create a three-column table with as many rows as you have current projects. Use the left-hand column to list the project names, the centre to describe the current status succinctly, and the right-hand column to detail forthcoming action. Here's a dummy extract:

Project	Status	Action
New client	Terms orally agreed	Get contract signed
Cost control	Identified problem	Arrange meeting
Induction course	Concept agreed	Draft structure
Operations review	In progress	PB to do by 4
Pricing plan	Proposal with Finance Department	JC to do by 9.12

Words are powerful tools, so know which to use and when. You wouldn't use a spade to chop down a tree. Get the meanings just right for maximum effect. An otherwise effective memo can be punctured by grammatical imprecision, and the most well-thought-out case can seem sloppy to a reader who is distracted by a spelling mistake or two. Use your computer's spell check to catch mistakes but don't rely on it entirely. Spell checks don't pick up 'grate' if you meant 'great'.

You may enjoy finding clearer, shorter words, and squeezing more meaning into fewer pages, and your readers may enjoy your work more. Gaining a reputation for being a good writer will help to get your work read, understood and acted upon, which is what you want.

Pictures can help too. One or two charts might show what you mean more clearly than several hundred words. Can you display the figures as a chart? Although charts can consume a lot of space, they may only require a few seconds of attention to be understood.

Written work normally needs supplementary action. If you put an hour's work into getting a written communication right, it's often worth spending five minutes calling the person you wrote, to see if they got the information: was it what they wanted and do they now need anything else? Don't just let it die. People tend to feel happier about something when they have been asked if they are happy about it. They value being consulted.

Judge the effectiveness of your written work not by whether people tell you it's good – although if they do, it usually is – but by whether it has the effect you intended. Did it work?

When Aeschines, a Greek orator, spoke, they said, 'How well he speaks.' But when his compatriot Demosthenes spoke, they said, 'Let us march against Philip.' Which was what Demosthenes wanted them to do. Write for effect, not affect.

Self Check

1. How effectively do you write?
2. Does your work have a beginning, middle and end?
3. Do you immediately identify the subject matter?
4. Do you identify clearly the action that needs to be taken?
5. Do you spell out the reasons why?
6. Do you communicate unambiguously?
7. Can you summarize the key points in under a page?
8. Do you need to add anything else?
9. Do you cut out redundant words?
10. Do you check your work carefully?
11. Will a chart show what you mean more clearly?
12. Can you use written words to persuade people to take action?

4.3 Figure it out

Figures have a deceptive simplicity

Someone once said to me, 'They could be oranges, they just happen to be numbers.' Numbers tell you about the scale and amounts of things.

Most executives receive masses of data. Computers can issue reams of figures on everything from budgetary projections to performance reports. If you look at every statistic that comes your way, you might do little else. The successful executive sifts the important numbers from the mass, and knows what to look for before looking at a set of tables.

Be clear in your mind what it is you want to know, which relationships are important, which variances would be significant. Financiers are in the habit of looking at the bottom line – so-called because it usually sits at the bottom of the page – which measures a company's profit (on a profit and loss table) or retained cash (on a cash flow table). Others look at the numbers themselves.

If you are looking at a table that's unfamilar, start by looking at what underlies the figures, namely the definitions and assumptions. These are often tucked away on a separate sheet at the back, or sometimes they are not present at all. You need to understand the definition of each line in any table before you give credence to the numbers. What has been included? What's excluded? How has inventory been treated? Most importantly, what are the sources: that is, how do we know the figures are correct?

When looking at future projections, or even contemporary projections where some of the relevant hard information is not yet available, the assumptions are crucial. If you believe them, the rest of the table will also be satisfactory – unless an arithmetical error has been made – but if you don't believe the assumptions on which the table is based, the figures will be wrong too. Save yourself time by studying the assumptions first.

You may be interested in many other things. It's obvious that numbers measure quantities but the absolute quantities are rarely important. It's the relative numbers that matter. In organizations, they can show whether there is more or less of something, for example, output, than we expected (which could suggest we should adjust our expectations), and whether there is more or less than enough of something, for example, income (in which case we may need to take action). Historic numbers tell us whether our margin is sufficient, sales are OK or our costs are higher than we need them to be. Projections tell us what someone else thinks, but don't believe other people just because they use numbers instead of words.

Numbers tell us how things change. They are the best guide to the past, and the past is normally the best guide to the future. They show how the past has or hasn't been changing. They suggest how the future may or may not change.

It's a curiosity that some finance (and other) departments churn out numbers by the thousand. Having created the numbers seems to be a good enough reason to circulate them, but relatively little effort may be put into who needs to know what. Some produce and circulate numbers with great precision, like $7,583,208.61. Maybe they think the 61 cents is important? Was even the $208 significant? Quantities described in simplified numbers (in this case $7.58m) are more likely to be read and understood. Too much detail obscures.

The tables you receive may not tell you what you want to know, at a glance. If that's the case, decide which numbers you really need and tell the person who produces the table what you really want. The table producer may be labouring under the illusion that you want all this information, but to you it is actually unhelpful. Maybe the meaning would be much clearer if the figures were produced as a bar chart or a pie chart. All such things can spin off at the touch of a few buttons.

Most teams, divisions and organizations have only a handful of key numbers. Anyway, they couldn't possibly focus on and respond to any more. The fewer the numbers you focus upon, the greater their likely effect. Choose your key numbers with care. You may want to circulate them widely. The rest can remain the province of a numerate élite. What are the two or three numbers that are really important to your performance?

When you look at numbers, they may tell you something or nothing. That's what you want to learn. If the numbers show that something you have done didn't work, it's a good bet that if you do it again, it still won't work. It's seldom worth arguing with historic numbers. It's much better to take the point and change your behaviour. Numbers remorselessly show the gap between theory and reality, and can help you to face that reality. By changing your behaviour, you turn yesterday's numbers into history.

Numbers can show if the near past is better than the far past. They can tell us whether there is more or less of something than in the previous time period. They can show trends and can highlight the unexpected. They show when surprising things happen. They tell us when we need to change our expectations of the future.

People use numbers to project what might happen in the future. It's tempting to show the result that we want. How can it be challenged? True, it hasn't happened, but it hasn't failed to happen either. It's in the future. All projections merely show what someone or some team believes about the future, which doesn't mean you should believe that it will happen. Instead of looking at the figures – which just might be only the ones that someone wants you to see – challenge the point of view. What evidence is there that they are right? What happens if they are not? How much (how little) do you have to vary them before you would be in serious trouble if you went ahead on this basis? How much room for error do you have?

Some executives want to show that the future will be successful. They are unlikely to put up bad figures unless they have already reconciled themselves to killing the project, and nine times out of ten, they won't kill what they have started to create. They are more concerned about showing the result they want than the possible consequences of the future turning out somewhat differently. I have seen people latch on to a few months' growth as an opportunity to project good long-term growth. They know the result they want to achieve, and the projections are a means they will bend to their end. These people are dangerous. They use numbers for support not illumination. They are trying to sell you something that probably won't exist. One way to spot them is to insist on seeing a comparison of their past projections with the *actualité*. You may well find that they didn't predict the present accurately. They thought it would be better than it is – and they now think the future will be good. You are the hurdle that stands between them and the pit. Careful, they may pull you in on their way past.

It's hard to project well. You need a fearless desire to get it right. You are hunting for the truth, whatever it may bring. Look at what has happened in the past. Did we achieve our previous projections? If not, were we over-optimistic in our forecast? Or was there a failure of implementation? If so, what will be different about the execution this time? If nothing is different, why would we get a different outcome next time? If you do the same things, you are likely to get the same results.

You have to put the truth before any preconceived notion of what you think the truth should be. Do you really want to bend the truth to fit your current view of the world? Or would you rather extend your view to embrace the truth, before it takes you by surprise?

Self Check

1. Can you use numbers to see the relationship between things?
2. Can you see the shapes that numbers can conjure up?
3. Can you see how they move together and apart?
4. Can you sort the useful numbers from the rest?
5. What are the three or four numbers that are most important to you?
6. Are you receiving the numbers you really need?
7. Who needs which key numbers?
8. Do you use charts to illustrate the point you want to make?
9. Do you usually achieve the projections you make?
10. If not, what are you going to do differently?

4.4 Make a good first impression

Start as you mean to go on

Most people make a snap judgement of the people they meet in well under a minute. Your fate may be decided in fifteen seconds.

Think of someone important you met for only a moment or two. What were your impressions? You may have noticed their appearance: the face, posture and clothes. The words spoken may have left less of an impression than the tone of voice and the handshake.

We make our preliminary judgements of people unconsciously, based upon the similarity of their characteristics to other people we have met and known. We don't even need to recall the people to make the link. It's an experience-based judgement.

Some people get their strongest impression of another at the moment that hands are shaken. They are tactile. At that moment, you want to be sure you are thinking the right sort of thoughts about the person you are meeting. Thoughts may be sensed. Incidentally, it's absolutely worthwhile ensuring that your hands are clean and fresh to the touch, and that you give a firm but not crushing handshake. Some people give such firm handshakes that you don't remember anything else. You wouldn't want to shake that hand again.

Like it or not, appearances are important. They aren't the only factor that influences people, or even the most important, but in the initial stages of a relationship there is little else to go on. I think that most people mean more by 'appearance' than the physical demeanour. They mean their sense of a person. Take some time before your next important meeting to check your appearance. Make it routine.

Think back to a time when you made a good impression. What did you feel? What did you do? How did you move? How did you breathe? How did you stand? How did you move your hands?

Typically, we think, feel, and maintain a particular body posture when we make a good impression. Are you willing to try a little experiment? Stand up, with your legs a little bit apart. By all means carry the book with you. Now push your shoulders slightly up and back, push your head up so you are looking twenty degrees above the horizontal, and smile. Once you are doing that, try to feel unhappy. Difficult, eh? One way to help to reproduce a good impression is to move the way you move when you usually create a good impression.

Make time to get yourself into a good state before a meeting. You won't be able to do this if you arrive at a place in a great hurry. Instead arrive early, allow yourself a moment or two, think about the people you may meet and how you want those meetings to go.

Make sure you have a supply of your business cards with you. Keep and collect the business cards you receive. You may find it useful to make a note of the date on which you met someone on the back of their card. In conjunction with your diary, you then have a system for recalling when you met someone and at what meeting. Better still, put each new contact into your database. Now you can develop your relationship easily.

Self Check

1. What makes a good first impression in your eyes?
2. What sort of qualities do you look out for in the people you meet?
3. What tends to put you off?
4. What sorts of first impression do you typically receive?
5. What sort of first impression do you usually make on other people?
6. How do they respond to you?
7. How do you feel when you make a good impression?
8. What do you do that may help to make a good impression?
9. Can you make that part of your standard 'meeting new people' routine?

4.5 Make a good second impression

Successful executives have good relationships

Don't just try to make a good first impression. Keep on making a good impression come what may.

First impressions of people are sometimes revised. As you begin to interact, people consider things like: does this person listen to me – is she interested in understanding my point of view – does she appreciate it?

Many executives are more anxious to get their points across than they are to understand the point of view of the person they have recently met. They want to show before they want to be shown. They are interested only in themselves. When two such people encounter each other, the meeting can be long and arduous. It's as vital to make time to listen as it is to have something to say.

Keep up the courtesies at work. You don't need to spend much time having coffee in a rest room, but you can ask after people and listen to them. Are there any people at work with whom you don't get on? A bad relationship is a luxury most executives can't afford. It's likely to trip you up from time to time. People you don't get on with can have a habit of passing on their opinion to others. That can be very costly and difficult to counter effectively, since you don't know quite what they have said to whom. The best way to deal with the problem is to straighten the relationship out. You probably won't do this by trying to get the other person to understand your point of view. If you do, he will probably try and get you to understand his point of view. Fine – but neither of you is listening to the other.

If you try going to the person and hearing them out you may find that the other person has grounds for being upset with you. If so, you could offer an apology and begin to deal with the problem. Once you have heard the other person out, they may be able and willing to reciprocate by listening to you. Which might have been your first priority.

You may or may not want to do business with your friends, but you do want your business relationships to be friendly.

Self Check

1. How do you develop your business relationships?
2. How do you get to know and understand people better?
3. If you don't listen to them, why would they listen to you?
4. Do you try to keep in touch with people?
5. Do you try to develop good relationships in work?
6. Are there any bad relationships which you could improve?

4.6 Meet with people

Meetings are a means to an end

A meeting is two or more people communicating in the same

93

room. It is also more than each of them talking. It involves listening, which means being open to new information.

Some people go to meetings determined to do anything except meet with the other people. What they really want is to sound off. They want to be heard. Or they want to win. Or they want to sound important. (This is too often the case.) The last thing they want to do is really meet someone. For one thing, if you meet someone, you might change.

Perhaps more time is consumed in meetings than in any other single business activity, and much of that is wasted. Meetings are unproductive when we don't prepare, when we talk too much and listen too little, and when we don't follow through afterwards.

Some meetings lack an agenda, a chairman and meeting papers. They may even lack a clear purpose. It takes a heroic effort to rescue a meeting which is set up like this. Never start a meeting that doesn't have an agenda without at least asking for one. When the purpose is unclear a lot of irrelevant hot air may be expended to no apparent purpose. Over-talking also occurs when participants lose sight of the objective of the meeting, if they ever had sight of it in the first place, or if the chairmanship is weak.

Some people enjoy meetings for the meeting's sake. For them, a meeting is not a means to an end, it is an end in itself. It is an end to be enjoyed, so the process is secondary. After all, a meeting is an opportunity to meet with other people and have them listen to you, which encourages some people to appreciate their own importance.

If you think a meeting may be unnecessarily long, try asking at the beginning, or even before you turn up, for a scheduled finish time. If you don't have a finish time, how will you be able to plan any activity to follow the meeting? Imagine you invited some people to a meeting and you didn't tell them in advance when it would finish. Would you expect them to be able to stay all day? Would you expect them to clear their diaries and stay until it is finished? If so, hadn't you better tell them?

In fact, every organization's meetings should have a start time, a latest finish time, a list of who is going to be there and an agenda. All of which easily fits on one piece of paper.

In real life, meetings are part of a process. They have a purpose. They are a means to an end, not an end in themselves. They cannot be purposeless, any more than any other part of executive life can be purposeless and survive.

A business meeting is only likely to be successful if at least one of the participants has prepared for it – someone needs to know what the meeting is about. Someone also needs to know what would represent a successful meeting, otherwise no one may ever know if the meeting was successful. That means thinking about what needs to be done, before it takes place. Otherwise it's the blind leading the blind.

Who knows the facts about the subjects that are to be discussed? Can they be committed to paper and circulated in advance so that they can be considered carefully? Would the author need to be at the meeting? What kind of decision needs to be made? If decisions need to be made at the meeting, who needs to be party to them, in other words, who needs to be there? If the purpose of the meeting is simply to share information does it really need to happen? Could you cancel it? Might it be better simply to circulate a note? As a rule, don't invite people along just so they feel involved. They may not want to waste their time either.

Apparently useful and fluent meetings may still be a complete waste of time if no behaviour changes in consequence, and no action follows. That's why making a note of agreed actions, who will do them and when, is a powerful discipline. If a task has been identified but it hasn't been allocated to anyone, it's relatively unlikely to be done. If it is allocated to someone but no date is agreed for completion of the task, each person may have a different impression of when it will be done, or perhaps no impression at all. If no one else is making such notes, the successful executive is likely to do so, if only because it makes the time invested, in the form of attendance at the meeting, more worthwhile.

Prepare for each meeting you attend and before you go, and think about the papers you might require when you get there. How often have you got to a point in a meeting when you realized you didn't bring a document to which you should now refer? Public failure looms. Putting your papers in an order which corresponds with the agenda will make them easier to access. Is it likely that you will need your diary for when a following meeting is scheduled? Or will you just hope that you will happen to be free?

If you have access to one, take a lap-top with the relevant files on disk. You may want to arrive in good time to sit near a power point so your flex can feed off the mains. It could be a long meeting.

Some people in some companies are regularly late for meetings. Perhaps they don't clear their desks or block all calls from five minutes before the meeting starts; perhaps they don't allow sufficient time to get to the meeting; or they've forgotten the meeting until you call them from the phone in the meeting room. Perhaps they like making a grand entrance. To most organized executives, habitual lateness looks undisciplined, discourteous or both. Can you think of the people who are habitually late? (If your own name comes up, remember you can change.)

Successful executives get to meetings on time. They also know why they are there. One way to be on time is to make a habit of going five or ten minutes early. Take some papers with you so you won't lose any waiting time. You can sit in the room quietly attending to your own business, and others may be pleased to see you as they arrive. If you are held up for a minute or two on your way to the room, you can still get there in time. The successful executive will have scanned the agenda in advance, possibly at the beginning of the week, and thought about what the meeting should achieve.

A meeting is an opportunity to get value from others. One of the goals of a successful executive is to understand what the other people at the meeting are trying to achieve, and elicit any views they may have. Try to make sure you listen to these before pressing your own views. This might sound soft, but it tends to be effective. People turn out to be more receptive to the views of someone whom they sense has been listening to them.

Make notes of others' views and suggested actions as they are made. You could make an entry of the subject and date of the meeting in your notebook. Use subheadings to group your notes for easy reference rather than just pouring them out. Think about what is being said. Refer back to your notes during the meeting, to sense the direction it is taking.

Consider whether someone should produce meeting notes for all parties and circulate them afterwards. If you think so, but no one is doing it, you could raise the issue. Or ask whether people would like you to take notes. If you do, they will probably say yes. One reason I like to take notes is that I tend to end up with a better understanding of what is happening. If I decide to make a note of every decision made – as I am likely to do – and then notice that after a long period of time, I haven't made a note of anything, I have learnt something. Nothing is being decided. Another thing I can do is keep the meeting notes mercifully succinct.

If no one else is acting as chairman, you may be able step into the role informally without treading on other people's toes. Look for angles that haven't been explored. Ask questions of everyone else rather than state a conclusion of your own. This is a good way to approach meetings anyway. Some studies have suggested that people who tend to ask questions exercise more influence in meetings than people who simply state their own conclusions. As chairman, you should follow the direction the meeting is taking and even try to anticipate the conclusions. Can you see a consensus developing? Is it the right consensus? Does another question need to be lobbed in to change the direction? If it's a consensus, have you actually been through the issues, or just skated around them?

Participating in a meeting is quite different from writing a report. A meeting is interactive, while a report is passive. A meeting is consensual, while a report is likely to be directive. People who read a report may well be pleased to know what you think and to accept your conclusions, but people at a meeting are more likely to want to participate themselves – which doesn't mean you can't have your say too, but you can state your ideas in a way which invites other people's opinions rather than as categorical truth. For instance, rather than say, 'We should do this . . .' you can say, 'Do you think it would be a good idea if we were to do this . . . ?' The former is a statement which provokes agreement or disagreement which can get people into fixed positions; the latter is a question which encourages others to come to their own view. If it turns out to be a bad idea, it's easy for you to move on. You don't have to retreat or apologize.

Be less concerned with your own agenda, which anyway evolves as the meeting continues, than ensuring that the meeting gets the maximum value from everyone who attends. If they all leave feeling they had a chance to participate, and agreed with the conclusions, they will be much more committed to the ensuing plan of action. Without that commitment, no behaviour may change, and the meeting was probably a waste of time.

Meeting reports are vital. It's seldom worth circulating a note of everything that was said. Don't commit hot air to paper – people are too busy to read back over everything, and they already had one chance to listen. However, it often helps to circulate a note of who is supposed to do what and when. Your organization may have its own style of meeting reports. One way to produce them is to list the action points in the main body of the document and reserve the right-hand column for the initials of the person who is going to undertake the action and the date by which the task is due to be completed. Like this:

Project Pineapple Meeting Report, 6.12.

Item	Action
Final financial forecasts to be prepared	AT 12.12
Distribution plan to be revised	JF 13.12
Issue brief to suppliers	RT 14.12
Call software company	NS 12.12

The briefer the better. You could emphasize the dates by giving them a column of their own. If you are issuing paper reports, highlight people's initials on their own copy.

Self Check

1. How effective are you in meetings?
2. Do you check which documents you may need at each meeting?
3. What about a calculator and a diary?
4. Do you turn up to meetings on time?
5. Do you check to see if there is an agenda and make sure you understand it?
6. Do you make sure you know when the meeting is scheduled to finish?
7. Do you tend to state your views categorically or ask questions?
8. Do you know which points you want to get across?
9. Do you try and get the meeting back to the point when it seems to have wandered off it?
10. Do you try to ensure that each task is identified and allocated?
11. Do you make clear notes of the decisions and action points?
12. Do you check to see if the action points were carried out?

4.7 One to one

One and one makes three

Much of an executive's work is done one to one, whether in person, on the phone or in writing. One to one communication is different partly because there is no audience. It's just the two of you, so you can combine in whatever way the two of you choose, as no one else is there to stop you. Neither of you is openly or covertly communicating with other parties, you are simply trying to communicate with one another and maybe combine your minds to reach a solution that neither of you might have managed to reach on your own.

More important, you have a chance to listen properly to

the other person. Also, you can see how the other person responds to your ideas much more closely than you might manage in a bigger meeting. Mostly, we notice the face: a smile or frown is obvious. But how is the other person sitting? Leaning away from you or towards you? And what about their eyes? Do they show interest, concern or are they glazing over? If you think you are losing the other person because they seem to be thinking about something else, ask them what they think of what you have just said. If they have lost interest, you will bring them right back; if they are thinking about something you said a few moments ago, they will probably tell you. If they suspect their distraction has been noticed, they may work harder to stay with what you are saying.

You want to understand the person with whom you are meeting. Listen closely. What are they thinking about? What's on their mind? What do they want to achieve? How could they be helped? How does that affect what *you* want to achieve?

What you say may be important, but it may not be as important as the way you say it. Being right may or may not matter. The effect of your words in the way you deliver them does matter. So does the effect of the other person's words. Are you open to them? Are you open to the idea that the other person might have something to say that you hadn't anticipated?

Even with just two people present, it's almost always worth thinking about the meeting beforehand. What is its purpose? What do you want from the other person? If you are asked why you are having the meeting, or what input you want to get from the other person, would you be able to answer concisely? Do you have a purpose in mind, or are you just going through the motions? If you can't think of a good purpose, maybe you should check why the other person wants the meeting. If they don't know either, maybe you could both save time by cancelling it.

You want to interact with the other person, which means listening deeply and closely. As the meeting continues, ask yourself: what do they really want from the meeting? Remember, you already know what you want. What are they really trying to achieve here? How could you help them?

Maybe it's something quite different from the purposes you had in mind. No matter. Things crop up. You can be flexible enough to handle them.

The end of the meeting is equally important. You are likely to have made a note of what seem to be the action points as you go along. You can use this to help you to summarize the action points concisely as the meeting draws to a close: 'Let me see if I understand correctly what we are going to do . . .' In fact, going over the action points can be a good way to conclude a meeting which you feel may otherwise drag on relatively unproductively.

Chance meetings can be useful too, even though you can't always prepare for them. Maybe you see someone in the corridor or at the coffee machine who could be helpful. Because you have already done your daily planning, you know that you want to see that person, and you can probably remember what you needed to see them about. Nevertheless, you may want to be careful how you approach the encounter. Maybe it isn't appropriate to talk in any depth now. Maybe you would be better to settle for making an appointment to talk later in the day: 'Hi John, we need to talk about the banana project, when would be a good time to meet?'

Self Check

1. How well do you listen one to one?
2. Do you make yourself aware of what the other person really wants?
3. Can you figure out their purpose?
4. Do you listen to the whole person or just the words that are actually said?
5. Do you listen for their feelings?
6. How much effort do you make to understand their agenda?
7. Do people you meet feel you understand them?
8. Do you notice how people respond to your ideas?
9. Do you spot the narrowing of the eyes that may register concern?
10. Do you notice when people have a problem with what you have said?
11. Do you stop to bring the problem out, or sail on regardless?

4.8 Present persuasively

Present a picture

At some time or other, executives present information to clients or suppliers, staff or bosses, or simply other team members. Whether you are presenting to five people or five hundred, the object of most presentations is to cause a particular point of view to be taken and a consequent decision to be reached.

Even if you are not sure that you will enjoy presenting, you do want to get your message across. Even if it's simply educating an audience, it's something you believe in. In essence, the task is to tell the truth as you see it.

Think first of the effect that you want to have. What is the outcome you want to achieve? What should people think when they leave your presentation? You may need to recommend what should be done, and give your reasons. Usually, this can only work if you are familiar with the topic and have explored it closely enough to be reasonably sure that your recommendations are correct. Inadequate work can rarely be papered over in a corporate environment.

Start with what you want people to have before the presentation. What is it they should understand before they come along? Are there papers they should read? Is there some thinking you want them to have done? Do they already understand the purpose of the presentation? If not, do you still have time to tell them? You may want them to have thought through the problem, as you see it, before they come along, then you can use the presentation to provide the answer. Or you may want to provide background information. While some people may not study it, others who attend your presentation may be reluctant to agree with you until they have read the background. The 'leave-ahead' document can smooth the way.

While you are preparing for the presentation, think about what you want people to take away from it when it's finished. Do you want them to have an opportunity to re-read the material afterwards? Are you sure that they will make up their minds, in which case you may not want to give them anything. The mission is already accomplished. Some people put more time into the 'leave-behind' document – writing, editing, commenting, rewriting, printing, photocopying, and binding – than they do into preparing for the presentation itself. This is almost always a mistake. A short 'leave-behind' document, a copy of the slides, or a short personal letter, may have as much, or more, impact.

Like most other communication, a presentation needs shape. Specifically, it needs a beginning, a middle and an end. As the saying goes, you need to tell them what you are going to tell them, tell it to them, and then tell them what it was you told them. Some say that after that you must get them to tell it to you to see if they got it, and then tell it to them again if necessary. Most people won't hear most of what you say. On average people are likely to remember only about a third of what they hear, which is one reason for saying your key messages several times. If they don't hear you the first time, they may hear you the second time or the third. Use different words each time to get your message across.

Some people who turn up to a presentation aren't entirely clear why they are there. They may still be thinking about what they were doing before they left their office, or they may be contemplating dinner tonight. They may have remembered the subject matter but not whether or how they are supposed to contribute, so you have to find a way to get them involved and committed.

Is it a pleasure for you to be there? If so, you could tell them. Are there half a dozen of you present? You will want to introduce the team quickly. If everyone doesn't know everyone else, it's usually a good idea to give the audience a note of the names and job titles.

The bigger the audience, the stronger the case for starting with humour. Even in a small audience, laughter lubricates. Do find something to puncture the artificial nature of the event, something that will connect with the audience, something that will show them you are human. Build it into something that's just happened. Maybe something that occurred in the room a few minutes before or something that happened to you on your way to the speaking venue. Look for something that chimes in with today's event. It's an anniversary, a birthday, five years to the day after such and such, or maybe it's just a month from the end of your financial year. If you can't find anything else, maybe the weather is dull but you are going to provide some cheer. Tell them about you.

The less the audience knows you, the stronger the case for letting them know that you know something about them. Maybe they have achieved something notable recently. You could mention it. If they are your peers, perhaps you could congratulate them or tell them that you look up to them. If they are your bosses, maybe it's an honour for you to be there. You could tell them and then move swiftly on.

You may also be able to point to some things you have in common. I think one of the key questions most audiences ask themselves about a presenter is, 'Is this person one of us?'

It's like the 'Would we let someone into our tent?' question. You are trying to build rapport.

It will usually be helpful if you give the audience some idea of what it is you are going to do immediately after your introduction, for instance, 'We are going to review the alternatives open to us, look at the pros and cons of each of them, and then give you our recommendations.' That provides shape. Depending upon the quality of your relationship with the audience you may want to add something like, 'If you can't identify anything wrong with our analysis, we will ask you to support our recommendations.' Now they know exactly why they are present. You want their support, and they know the terms you propose – find out where we are going wrong or support it. You win if they support you but you also win if they can improve upon your recommendation. They are working with you and you have something stronger to take forward.

There's no need to get defensive if they take a different point of view. If you won't respect their point of view, why should they respect yours?

You'll have thought through what you want your audience to have in front of them while you are presenting. Bear in mind, it could distract them. I have seen meetings where copies of the slides with the key points were given to people at the beginning of the meeting with the request that they shouldn't look at the relevant slide until that point in the presentation had been reached, which of course they promptly ignored.

You may have put an agenda on the table in front of each of them which should include each presenter's name. So you might continue: 'You will see that each of the options is outlined in the agenda in front of you,' and then give people an idea of what they are supposed to do – do you want them to keep quiet? Should they make their own notes? – for example, 'Do contribute your ideas as we go along and feel free to make notes. We will supply a copy of the slides at the end of the presentation.' So far it's been easy going for the audience, but you are beginning to engage their minds.

That was just introduction. Now you can pause to get more attention and imprint your presentation's 'headline'.

Can you summarize the whole thing in a sentence or two? Can you find a powerful metaphor? Can you use some visual imagery? Punch a message home hard.

Once you are through that headline, you may focus on the objective. What is it you all want to achieve? What is the objective? What would a successful outcome be like? Now you can begin to look at the selection criteria. How would you choose one option over another? How would it manifest the desired qualities? How would they be obvious even at this stage?

Beginnings and ends are in some ways the most important, as that's where you are likely to get the highest level of attention. Concentration tends to dip in the middle. Oral communication is particularly difficult to do well because most people don't hear most of what's being said. You need to project your key messages more than once.

However good the delivery, a presentation requires good content. You are making an argument. You are trying to win people to a particular point of view.

You should start your preparatory work by getting your main message clear: what is it that you want to communicate? Then get the structure clear, then the main argument, and finally the content. It's best to compose an appropriate beginning and end only when the rest of the presentation is clear. You prepare the middle first.

You'll have to work out what visual support you need. For some people a powerful picture is more persuasive than a thousand words. So what would be the most powerful images you could use? Where will you find them? In what form should they be presented? Boards? Slides? Do you need the last minute flexibility of overhead transparencies?

Given the amount of work in most presentations, it may be worth sounding out the decision-maker(s) on the direction of your recommendations before you spend much time on what may be a dead-end. If you ask for advice, you had better be ready to take it. Or maybe you already have a pretty good idea of what could and couldn't be accepted.

It's also worth getting to understand the point of view of the audience. How much do they already know about what you are going to present? What is their mindset? What do you need to convince them of? Is there one particular obstacle to them coming round to your point of view? If so, can you hit that point hard? Maybe you can make it the main point of your presentation. Maybe you could agree with whoever is organizing the meeting – it may be you – that you will speak with some of the people beforehand.

Visit the room in which you are going to present as long as possible in advance. Five minutes may not give you sufficient time for manoeuvre. Check the layout. How far will your audience be from the screen? Where will you stand? It's usually worth having a good extension lead – existing power points can restrict your options. If you will need to refer to notes, where will you keep them? Get someone to stand in the position from which you intend to present and then go and sit where the audience will be. How does it look? How could you improve it?

Where will you be immediately before you start? How will you be introduced? How will you move to where you need to present? Will you be in the room before others arrive? Bear in mind that they will be forming their impressions of you from the moment they enter the room, whether you have started to present or not. Introduce yourself personally if you can. Find out more about them. What's on their mind? What do they want from the presentation. Why have they come?

Sometimes you will present as part of a team. What will the person before you have said? How will they pass over to you? Nothing has less impact than 'And now I am going to hand over to John Green.' Just do it. What would a good link be? Of course, rehearsals are vital. The more you rehearse, the better the presentation. Providing you keep trying, you will go on improving with each 'take'. For one thing, your timing will get better.

This is especially important when you use visual props. How will you knit together spoken word and visual message? You may want to use powerful pictures but you won't want them to distract the audience from you. You may find people listen closely to what you say when you introduce pictures effectively. For instance, say 'This shows the close relationship between . . .' just as you reach for the board or flick the remote, and now you are speaking the heading your audience is reading. You are showing them you know your material. You are putting it in context and telling them you have thought through what it means. You are in charge of the visuals, not the other way around. This only works if you have thought about the material and rehearsed it too. You need to know exactly what comes next.

You may get nervous before you pitch. Mainly, people are nervous that it may not go well. One way to minimize nervousness is to know your material well, having rehearsed it two or more times. Another is to envisage the meeting going well. If neither of these has worked sufficiently, there is one more thing you can do: breathe deeply. Tension tends to make our breathing shallow, which diminishes the supply of oxygen, which underpins the tension. Break out of it by breathing deeply.

You may need to use cue cards with key words to make sure you don't lose your way. Or you may know your material so well that they are unnecessary. Speaking without notes gives you more ability to listen to your argument and to sense what the audience thinks. It is also more exciting since you are never quite sure what is going to happen next.

Practise as much as you can. The more you practise, the better your presentation will be. Certainly your familiarity with the material increases, your pitch improves and your timing gets more nearly perfect. I know some executives who will run through whole presentations seven times over. Churchill practised in front of a mirror. Yet some executives decline to practise even in advance of potentially career-making presentations. Maybe they are too nervous. Maybe they are urgency addicts.

Think clearly about the message and the form will largely take care of itself, but you may want to get the first half dozen phrases word perfect. Practising the delivery will give you stronger turns of phrase.

Your voice is vital. It needs to be strong but not too strong. Again, breathing is crucial. If you don't breathe in fully, you are unlikely to project strongly. Your voice needs to be clear since some of your audience may not hear too well. Try to make sure you pronounce each word in a way that can be understood. Vary the tempo and the volume. Talk more quietly when you want to be more intimate, but louder to generate excitement.

Use your eyes when you present. Try to maintain as much eye contact as you can with the audience. They are looking at you. Try not to look at any one member of the audience for more than fifteen seconds or so, as it may make him or her uncomfortable. Looking at different parts of the audience from time to time will help you draw in other people before they drift off.

Use your body too. Move your arm to emphasize a point; move your whole body to re-attract attention, or move closer to get more intimate, but don't move constantly from side to side or in any other direction. It's too tiring for your audience.

People lose concentration easily, so vary the tempo. You can speed up and slow down. You can even stop. I was midway through a particular presentation when I felt myself losing my way and I came to a stop. Instead of panicking I just paused and thought about what should come next. The audience didn't walk out or even get restive. On the contrary, their concentration increased. They really wanted to know what would come next. So pause briefly at the end of each sentence and make a longer pause at what would be the end of a paragraph.

People don't need to hear you constantly. They need time to take things in. You need time to notice them. Are their eyes glazing over? Are you watching them? If I am too far away from an audience, I normally look to see if I can get a bit closer. Maybe you can dispense with the microphone.

Once you are near the end of the presentation, you need to tell them what it was you told them. You should summarize your case, taking account of any helpful interjections. This may be done by whoever began the presentation, so that the same person tops and tails.

End with a flourish.

Self Check

1. How do you present?
2. What is your style?
3. Do you make time to identify the goal of your presentation?
4. What does your audience already know?
5. What will they want to get out of the presentation?
6. Do you visit presentation rooms in advance?
7. Can you take control of the stage?
8. Do you tell people what's coming up?
9. What visual support would be most effective?
10. Do you rehearse your presentation?
11. Can you vary your volume level and still be heard?
12. Can you conclude powerfully?

4.9 Listen, do you want to know a secret?

The more you listen, the more you know

The most important skill an executive can possess is the ability to listen. On its own, listening achieves little, but without it, you will never really get to the bottom of any situation. You simply cannot learn (except by reading material like this), nor will you understand people. And then they won't bother to understand you.

Everyone loves a listener. Someone who will listen to them, not just to what they are saying. Someone who listens to the whole person, who appreciates and seriously tries to understand them. You can learn to listen. However well you listen, you can sharpen your listening skills. Usually, the more attentively you listen, the deeper your learning may be.

In one training exercise, a group of us were thrown together to resolve a problem. Almost everybody had a point of view and was keen to say what they wanted to say. Each wanted to make an original contribution, something that was different from everything that had gone before, otherwise, how would they contribute to the solution? Simply by listening to what was being said, and then summarizing the position or group of positions, I became *de facto* chairman. I was also the person that almost everybody wanted to direct their remarks towards because they knew I would listen to them, something they didn't know about anyone else.

You can think much more quickly than people can talk. Which means you can silently replay what people say almost as they say it, giving you two chances to 'hear' what is said. Listening to someone means more than just hearing the words they say. To see the person behind the words, listen with your eyes. You should maintain eye contact for several seconds at a time.

You may or may not find that other people want to talk in a particular meeting. There are a number of ways by which you might encourage them to do so. One way is to be silent. This is risky since others may be equally quiet, or they may talk about matters other than the ones you want to be discussed. Usually, a better strategy is to ask questions.

It's also the best way to reach agreement. You can ask three kinds of questions. I call them hooks, hows and wouldn't its. Hooks tend to begin with a 'Would you like ...?' after which you express the benefit. It could be whatever favourable outcome you have in mind: a reduction in costs, an uplift in business or a more flexible procedure. Once the objective is understood and agreed, your colleague is hooked into the same purpose. At this point, you can move on to the hows. For instance, 'Tell me, how does it work at the moment?' Hows can include whys, as in, 'Why do we do it that way?' Once the advantages and disadvantages of the present system are spelt out, you can move on to the wouldn't its as in, 'It would be a good idea if we could [express the benefits previously mentioned] at lower cost, wouldn't it?' And, having pushed for the 'yes', you are in a strong position to show just how your proposal will meet the needs of the moment.

Even when you may feel you really want to put your point of view forward, it is usually preferable to continue to listen to the other person. As a general rule, you should listen until you

111

are sure that you understand fully their point of view. Why are they saying what they are saying? What do they hope to get out of the meeting? To what kinds of things are they likely to agree?

It's often the case that the less keen we are to communicate our point of view, the keener others are to hear it, and the more they listen to it when it does come. Of course, when you do speak, you are able to take account of all that you have learnt while you were listening. You understand the other(s), so you are more likely to be able to speak in a way that is relevant.

You may find yourself in a meeting with colleagues who are not listening to each other, they are simply stating their own point of view. What can you do? Rather than introducing a third point of view, or attempting to reconcile the other two by finding a compromise which one or both parties may reject, you might be better to show them both that someone is listening to them. Try feeding back to each of them what they have said, in your own words, and ask them whether you have understood them right. It may be that you haven't understood correctly, or it could be that when they hear the thoughts they have expressed, but in your language, they realize they have omitted to say something which now needs to be added. However, the biggest benefit of this approach is that the other person may listen to your words in a way that he hadn't to his colleague's. After all, to 'win', each of the protagonists probably needs your support. They want to see where you are coming down. Actually, you aren't coming down anywhere. You are just exploring and understanding.

When you are listening to words, try listening to the person as well. How are they standing or sitting – towards you or away from you? What does that body posture tell you? When they get excited what are they are talking about – that may be what really interests them – and when does their enthusiasm drop? Do you notice when they fold their arms – normally a sign of insecurity – and wonder what it is that they are worrying about?

It's also important to listen to your own thoughts. What's running through your mind right now? Maybe you should let that thought process continue. Where is it likely to lead you?

If information is power, listeners are the most powerful people in the world.

Self Check

> 1. How do you listen to people?
> 2. Do you pay attention to what is said?
> 3. Or are you busy thinking of what you are going to say next?
> 4. Do you replay the words silently as the speaker goes along?
> 5. Do you try to understand the person behind the words?
> 6. Can you pick up feelings as well as words?
> 7. Do you create opportunities to listen by asking the right questions?
> 8. Do you ask 'would', 'how' and 'wouldn't it' questions?
> 9. Do you try to ensure you understand others before you pour forth?

4.10 Remember what you want

What you don't notice, you'll never remember

People like to be remembered. Right now you may not have a good memory for names or faces. You may feel embarrassed by not being able to remember someone's name and you don't want to advertise your ignorance by asking again. If this happens to you, it's time you made time to develop your memory skills. There are several steps in remembering.

The first thing is you need to note the information in the first place. Some people who think they can't remember something are absolutely right. They can't remember it because they never noticed it. If you don't hear someone's name you won't be able to remember it. So the first key to having a good memory is noticing the information you want to remember.

113

The second thing you need to do is to store the information. Your brain has the potential to store much more information than you could ever give it. Capacity isn't the problem. The intrinsic memorability or immemorability of what you give your brain is the limiting factor.

Suppose you meet someone and her name is Sue. You hear the name and you look at the face. There may be nothing in this Sue's face that makes her look particularly like a Sue. She could have been called Sarah and had just the same face. You can say her name once or twice to give yourself more opportunities to hear the name and associate it with the face as you hear it. This is likely to help a bit but it's still not particularly memorable.

You could associate this Sue in your mind with another Sue you already know, for instance you could make a mental picture of them shaking hands. This links one Sue to the other as though they were both in a file marked 'Sue'. You have associated the face with other faces with the same name. You are creating mind files.

As soon as you learn a little about Sue, you can put this information in the same 'file'. Suppose she is an artist with three children, two boys and a girl. Now you can see her in a painting overall, palette in hand, having just finished a picture of two boys and a girl. Picture her face clearly and that information is likely to be available to you the next time you see her. You have made the file on this Sue a lot bigger. A bigger file is easier to find. It will be a big bright blue needle in a pink haystack.

You can use the absurd to make the information you receive more memorable. Make an absurd metaphor of what you see and it is likely to come back to you relatively easily. If you need to telephone Michael about a speaking engagement, see a telephone wrapped around a microphone.

Writing down the information you've put into your short-term memory helps. Making a note of it gives you an extra chance.

Sometimes you may need to remember a list. Try making it memorable. You may be able to visualize each of the items on the list and link them to one another. If you need to fax Sue and meet with John, see your fax coming out of Sue's machine

114

saying meet with John, and so on. Or take the first letters of each word and make them into a mnemonic (Memory Never Ever Matches Old News Instantly Correct). Or go over the list again and again.

Self Check

1. Do you remember people's names fairly easily?
2. What techniques do you use to remember people's names?
3. How do you make the information you want to remember easier to remember?
4. Do you come back to the information you are trying to remember?

4.11 Direct opinions

Opinions are an unreliable form of knowledge

'There's a time to listen, and a time to keep quiet', might be a good maxim for some. We are all confronted by any number of opinions and reflections every day. We hear views with which we agree, and views with which we disagree. It can be tremendously tempting to add a note of agreement or correction.

Most of the time, we don't know the circumstances well. We may know less than the person who has given the opinion, and even they may have an incomplete view of events. Reaching conclusions without knowing the facts opens us up to the possibility of being wrong.

Even agreeing with someone when we don't really know the rights or wrongs may help to confirm them in a wrong view, while diving in to disagree courts disaster. They may be right. They may be wrong and need to discover it for themselves. Even if we are right, why proffer our views where they may not have a positive effect? In fact, they may not even be wanted.

Sticking our nose into someone else's work is usually a

115

mistake. Even worse, it invites them to stick their nose into our business. Does this mean all discourse is doomed? We can listen to others' opinions and simply ask ourselves what they mean. Why do they have that opinion? Why are they worked up? How could this situation have been prevented? We can listen deeply and learn from what others say.

We can ask questions. Why do you say that? Why do you feel that way? How do you think this problem has come about? What do you think we need to do about it? What do you think we need to do next? And so on until a solution begins to emerge. You can listen without agreeing or disagreeing. You can even enquire. When you ask others their views, you show respect for them. When you give your own opinions, you show respect for yourself.

You don't need to jump off the fence until you have looked at both terrains and checked its height! You can save your opinions for when they are needed. You can apply them directly to situations where they can make a difference. The less you speak out when you don't need to, the more you will be listened to when you do need to say something.

Self Check

1. Do you sometimes agree with people because you want to be nice to them?
2. Do you disagree with things that are said without understanding the context?
3. Do you sometimes find you need to retract your words fast?
4. Do you think more of what someone is saying now or of what you may say next?
5. Do you encourage other people to listen to you by listening to them?

4.12 Be computer literate

Technology is an opportunity to be more effective

We're in the middle of a communications revolution. Your

PC, or Mac, or lap-top computer is a powerful tool. Successful executives know how to use computers quickly and effectively. They harness the power of computers to achieve their objects.

Of course, the core skill is still typing. Once you can type as fast as you can think, your fingers can follow your thoughts. Typically, this is about five times as fast as you can talk. An alternative is to slow down your rate of thinking, so you aren't constantly losing thoughts as you work. You can enhance your typing speed by making sure you look at the screen as you type, rather than moving your eyes round the keyboard all of the time. If you can't, make some time as soon as possible to learn to touch type. Since the time saved will give you a very good return on the time you spend. You'll also spot any mistakes quicker because you will see them pop up on screen. Speed your typing even further by creating an autotext directory of the longer words and phrases you use most frequently.

You may already be adept at creating documents. You may be able to pre-format them so you can adjust the style almost without effort. You may have learnt dozens of fast commands that save you time every time you use your computer, and you may know how to produce well-designed documents with a minimum of fuss. If not, make some time available to familiarize yourself with all the time-saving quick commands. Have you set up a database for your contacts, and where's your Christmas card list? What about spreadsheets and project planners? And how good are you with graphics and clip art and paint box and flow charts, and so on? There's always more to learn, and each of these skills will increase your effectiveness and your speed, which you might often need. With the benefit of greater speed, you can move more quickly to forestall crises.

Make some time this month to learn some computer skills. In fact, make some time every month. If you don't know that you could use them, it may be that you don't know what's available. And if you aren't e-mailing regularly, you're about to get left behind. Your task is to commit time to learning more of these skills, time which will save you much more time later.

117

Self Check

1. Can you type as fast as you can think?
2. If not, how much does that slow you down?
3. What could you do to speed up your typing?
4. How many fast commands have you mastered?
5. Could graphics help you to get your message across?
6. Can spreadsheets give you more power?
7. How good are you at creating spreadsheets and project planners?
8. Are you e-mail literate?
9. If not, when are you going to join in?

Chapter Five

You Progress

5.1 Understand your boss

Successful executives manage their bosses

A good working relationship with your boss is invaluable. Without it, you're crippled. You may also have a limited shelf life. Every boss has a strong interest in getting on well with each member of his team, while you have an even stronger interest in getting on well with your boss.

You also want to help your boss to perform well. The subordinates of high-performing bosses tend to get promoted. Those of underperforming bosses tend not to get promoted – and when that boss is finally found out, there will probably be a new broom appointed. So watch out!

Trust makes effective communication possible. Without it, communication will be minimal. So your first priority is to gain your boss's trust. That means being interested, supportive and reliable. Incidentally, the extent to which you trust your boss need not limit the degree to which your boss trusts you. You can earn your boss's trust anyway.

Your boss may not be perfect, but then you aren't perfect either. Some bosses show their best faces to *their* bosses, not to you. In which case you may see them at their worst. This doesn't mean they don't have a better side, but you may have to look for it. By the way, how do the people who report to you rate you?

Suppose your boss seems to be consistently unreasonable. Other people probably see the boss the same way. Now suppose you go out of your way to build a good relationship. You may be the only person who does that. Do you think your boss won't appreciate having someone who offers respect?

119

Try to understand what your boss wants to achieve at work. What does your boss do well? What strengths can your boss contribute? How can you help them to be applied more fully?

What's your boss's perspective on the team's tasks and how you fit in? You should stay interested in the answers to these questions. They may change as your boss begins to trust you, sees you being effective in your work, and feels your relationship grow.

Make quite sure that you understand what is meant by your boss's words. Listen very closely, scrutinizing the words for meaning, and think fast to check that you understand what is being said. Initially, your main goal will be to show that you can do what is asked of you – on time every time, within budget and to a better than satisfactory standard. Show that you think your boss's views are more important than your own. After all, your boss probably thinks so.

If and when you disagree, your boss may be right. Don't assume that you have all the information. You might be wrong if you think a particular course of action is wrong. You can, however, ask why it's proposed and what purpose we are trying to achieve. You might then go on to say that if we had another way to achieve that outcome without some of the problems, would we want to pursue it? Be ready to speak if everyone is about to set off in the wrong direction because they don't have a piece of information that you do. Share it, as fast as necessary, in the right context. Be ready to change your point of view as you see new aspects to a situation.

When the work you do turns out not to be exactly what your boss really wanted – and until your communication is perfect there will be such occasions – you won't take it amiss but will redouble your efforts to make sure that you understand exactly what the boss has in mind.

Bosses are often criticized by people who don't see the whole picture. Either stand up for your boss quietly but patiently if you hear criticism, or just say nothing. You don't need to be incredibly supportive, gentle support will do. Your boss is likely to hear about your support, but any tendency to amplify criticism jeopardizes your relationship. You can't control whether and when such behaviour will get back to him. Would you trust people who speak ill of others when their backs are turned? What do they say about you?

As your boss's trust in you increases, you will find a ready ear for your own views. You will be able to speak clearly and directly in a way which reflects your boss's agenda. As this cycle of listening carefully and responding precisely continues, you are likely to get more interesting projects. Your boss will be interested in your views. After all, you listen too. You'll begin to anticipate what your boss would want from a particular situation, so your influence will increase. You'll be able to take bigger decisions. Your boss is likely to support your work strongly and may even think of you as a protégé. Your boss will want you to shine. You may become a natural successor. That may not be the point, but it's a not unwelcome result.

What goes for your boss goes for your other colleagues too. Behave as well to them as you do to your boss, and your working relationships will blossom. Be trustworthy.

Self Check

1. Do you understand what your boss wants to achieve at work?
2. Do you listen carefully to what your boss has to say?
3. Do you understand what's really wanted when your boss asks you to do something?
4. Do you seek to understand your boss's views properly when you disagree?
5. Do you give your boss the benefit of the doubt?
6. Do you stand up for your boss when you are in others' company?
7. Do you stand up for others who aren't present too?
8. What could you do to improve your relationship with your boss?

5.2 A difficult colleague

When you have a problem with a colleague, it's your problem

From time to time, you may come across someone who seems difficult to work with, someone who doesn't seem to be well disposed towards you. Your words don't have the usual positive effect on them, and they clearly don't think highly of you. Before long, you start to notice their faults, which begin to grate. Maybe you discuss them with someone else to see if they have noticed the same faults. Now you wonder whether the person you are discussing is talking about you in similar terms.

You get along well with most people so you might think you aren't the problem. You may even find other people have had a difficult experience with the same person. The finger points towards them, so you think they are the cause.

Neither of you may have made time to get to know the other, opportunities to be courteous to one another may not have presented themselves, and now there's a lack of trust. The relationship seems to be going backwards. What can you do to turn the relationship around?

You can go out of your way to be positive towards this person. You can treat them at least as well as you would treat anyone else. They may be suspicious at first, and think it's some kind of trap and not respond. No problem. Fixing these things takes time. You just go on behaving well towards them. Subtly, and over a period of time, a superficial problem will evaporate as surely as water in the sunlight.

Maybe there is a deeper problem. Perhaps they feel you have slighted them in some way. You may have neglected to respond to an idea they put forward. You may have opposed them at a crucial moment and they may have taken it personally. You may have been critical about them and they may have overheard what you said or heard it through some third party.

What can you do? One approach is to let the problem

fester, but this is dangerous and could result in serious difficulty in future. Alternatively, you can go to them and ask whether something you have done, perhaps inadvertently, has upset them. Don't do this until you have done the interior work necessary to really want to get on well. I have seen people get together, ostensibly to sort out a problem between themselves, and all they have done is restated their positions more and more forcefully.

They may say you haven't upset them and ask you why. You may respond gently, by saying that you would value having a good working relationship with them and aren't sure whether there is some hesitancy on either side. If your colleague continues to say that there isn't a problem you can ask to be told if you ever do upset them in any way. Then the onus is on them.

Or perhaps they begin to tell you about a problem which may or may not be the one you had in your mind. Whatever they say, hear them out. You should also show them that you have heard and understood what they have said by restating the key points in your own words, for instance, 'So when I dropped the idea you felt I hadn't considered it carefully and that upset you.' Now you understand the problem you are in a position to start to rebuild the relationship, but you may have to begin by apologizing. Are you good at apologizing? Successful executives apologize handsomely.

What if the problem is with your boss? Suppose your boss regularly behaves badly towards you and others. The first thing you can do is recognize that this one is your boss's problem, not yours. Don't tackle your boss at the time of any bad behaviour, unless you are absolutely sure of your ground. Much better to do so when you are both calm. Even then, trying to tackle the problem head on is unlikely to work. You might instead focus on a related matter, for example, staff morale, and see what your boss thinks could be done to improve things. You might put the problem in your terms.

If you did something to earn a rebuke perhaps revisit the subject and confirm your apology. Words like 'I was wrong', can work wonders. Having admitted that much, you might ask your boss quietly to draw it to your attention if you do anything similar in future. In time, your boss may reflect your good behaviour back to you.

Self Check

1. Do you have a problem with a colleague?
2. Do you know what has caused the problem?
3. How could you find out?
4. What could you do to straighten out that problem?
5. Would you be willing to hear the person out?
6. Do you have enough courage to apologize?
7. Are you any good at apologizing?
8. Might some practice help?

5.3 Trust the future

The future is a huge opportunity waiting to happen

Successful executives trust the future. You don't need to be scared by it. 'Trust and be not afraid,' says St John's Gospel. The future could be a lot better than the present and probably won't be much worse. Anyway, you can influence the future. You don't need to wait for worry to do its worst, you can step free now.

Worry is like rust, it corrodes the future, but you can polish up your act. If you let it, fear eats away until it has its victory. Worrying is not enjoyable. Worry paralyses. Too often, worry is the cause of so many other problems.

Worry is a response. But the scale of the response, or even the appropriateness of it, is in question. Worry seems to be semi-detached from the world, because one person's worry is another person's spur to action. Fear of crime may diminish even when crime increases, or increase even when it is falling. Sometimes fear and events do move together, but that may be mere coincidence.

A man once faced a lot of problems. He was asked if he would like to visit some people who had no problems. On replying enthusiastically that he would, he was whisked away to visit a graveyard and realized that the living will always face challenges. That's part of the human condition.

5.4 Keep your head in a crisis

Crises force necessary changes

'If you can keep your head when all about you are losing theirs and blaming it on you', why then, Kipling might have added, you are a successful executive.

In some businesses, a crisis is never far away. They may be useful. Some years ago I was describing some difficulties to a friend. He said, 'That sounds like a crisis.' I said, 'That's right, it's a crisis.' He said, 'Good.' I was dumbfounded. He went on, 'In a crisis you have to grow.'

Crises can catapult you forward. They blow away the inertia that left you standing on your comfortable little island. The only question is whether you sink or swim.

Crises test even the best-run business, and the temptation to run around like a headless chicken is too great for some. If you can keep your head in a crisis you may be able to do a great deal of good. You might manage to resolve the crisis and learn from it.

Recently, a nephew and I found ourselves in a queue of cars which had slowed down to go past a bale of hay near the middle of the road. I started saying to Richard, 'We should . . .' intending to add 'stop and see to it,' but the man in the car in front of us did so. The point that this story demonstrates is that crises are the outcome of unresolved issues. The bale is an unresolved issue. It doesn't matter who caused the crisis. Until it's moved, everyone has to slow down. Sooner or later, someone will deal with the crisis. When the man in front got back into his car, having moved the bale to the side of the pavement, he was happy. He probably didn't move it in order to feel happy, he may have done it because it seemed the right thing to do, but his happiness was one of the outcomes of his action.

Crises test your faith in your plans, your company, even yourself. If, when a crisis erupts, people lose their nerve, you have two problems. One is the crisis. The other is that colleagues have lost their balance. They may no longer know what effect their own actions will have. They may strike out thoughtlessly and make things worse or they may be paralysed.

In some crises the most important thing you can do is to stay calm, or allow yourself to calm down, so you can see things clearly. You have a chance to find the best, or least bad, way out of the crisis. And when you are calm you can get purposeful too.

Look dispassionately at the worst thing that can happen. (But don't look at it for too long!) Then focus on the action that could be taken to avoid that happening. As soon as you have an action plan you have a way out. The next question is how much time do you have to find a better way out?

Self Check

1. How do you behave in a crisis?
2. Can you get calm even when others aren't?
3. Do you notice when you are upset and take steps to recover your calm?
4. Can you look at the situation dispassionately?
5. Can you see clearly enough to find a way ahead?
6. If not, can you find somewhere quiet to think?
7. What does that crisis tell you about your procedures?
8. What does the crisis reveal about what could have been done differently?
9. How would you change your behaviour in future?
10. What happens if you start changing that behaviour now?

5.5 Have a mission

Missions make people unstoppable

Many people do not seem to have much idea what their lives

are really about. And if *they* don't know, then probably no one else knows for them. They're just getting by. They wake up, have breakfast, go to work, do their work, go home, see friends or family, have supper, go to bed. Then they retire. They are killing time.

There's a vacuum where their mission should be. In times gone by, this might not have mattered so much. Indeed, in many earlier societies you couldn't choose what you would do, or even how you would do it. You did what your parents did, daughters like mothers, sons like fathers. You had a sense of place and you were stuck with it, for better or worse. Now there's an opportunity and a space.

Today, you can choose what you do and where you work. You can choose your own values and the contribution you make. You can make your mark in this world. You could write down your mission in the form of a statement. It could refer to your family, your work, and your community or country. It may encapsulate how you would like to be remembered by each of them. You don't have to work out the meaning of life itself or even the purpose of anyone else's life. They can sort themselves out. The challenge is to focus on your own.

It's absolutely possible for anyone to think about what their life could, should or will be about, but it's relatively unfamiliar territory for most people. It takes effort, quiet and stillness. You need to banish the daily bustle to get some perspective. You must let the dust settle before you open your eyes, let alone see clearly.

The most effective people have thought about this. They may not have done it in words, it may not be written into their personal organizer, but they have a sense of it. It is this mission that gives them their focus. It both energizes them and prevents them from being lured into blind alleys which don't further this mission.

Life speeds by. The only question is how you live it. Close your eyes and dream.

Self Check

> 1. What fulfils you?
> 2. What is your life about?
> 3. What would you really like to achieve in your life?
> 4. What sort of contribution would you like to make?
> 5. How do you want to contribute to family, community and work?
> 6. How would you want to be remembered?

5.6 Welcome criticism

Of thine own self, be critical

You may not usually welcome criticism. After all, what good does it do to have your weaknesses highlighted, especially in front of others? Anyway, nobody's perfect.

Criticism, however, can be a powerful key to self-improvement. If we could see ourselves as other people see us, we could do something about what they see, but while we don't, we can't. If we stick to a perfect view of ourselves, we are unlikely to make much progress.

It's easy to be sensitive to criticism. We may suspect it's a personal attack and that more is coming, and may look for ways to counter-attack to deflect it. This hardly works wonders for personal relations! A better strategy is to say nothing, listen, and keep breathing.

We don't have to take criticism personally. We can side-step any personal element in the criticism and just let it go by. We can learn from it. Maybe we will just learn about how someone feels. Maybe we will discover that we upset them. Maybe they will tell us about a problem that is really theirs.

When we take criticism personally, we are unlikely to accept it, much less learn from it. It's just someone else's opinion, and we can decide they are wrong. Even if they are wrong, the fact that they have given that opinion should reveal something.

You may even manage to thank them for it. Giving criticism isn't easy. The person who is criticizing you may really be quite scared. They may have had to steel themselves to confront you. They probably have a pretty good reason to do so. You need to understand it.

When we reject criticism, we tell the person who has given the criticism that we don't accept the opinion. We are saying to someone that they will have to try harder to get their criticism through, and they probably will.

Maybe it's worse. Perhaps we hear the criticism and immediately search our brains to find some way to criticize them equally forcefully. Maybe we try to think of something more wounding and think that might deter them in future. If so, we are saying that we will attack someone who criticizes us, and that we would rather damage the relationship than accept criticism.

It may not be correct to accept the criticism either. Fine. Just note it. Accept that it has been made sincerely and mull it over. That doesn't mean it's right to criticize others. Bite your tongue. Hold back. Watch what's happening. See if you can understand why it's happening. See if you can deduce what's causing the behaviour, and see if you can do something about that.

Simply putting the lid back on the kettle may create more noise. See if you can turn down the gas.

Self Check

1. Was anybody who criticized you ever right?
2. Did you let them know?
3. Do you regularly reject criticism before you have considered it?
4. Do you even counter-attack the person who has criticized you?
5. Can you watch the criticism without making a response?

5.7 Catch good ideas

Ideas need a mind to invite and receive them

How many interesting ideas have you heard? How many of them have you implemented? How many of the rest can you even remember?

You hear an interesting thought, reflect on it and then forget it. It's gone and you didn't make anything of it. Maybe one day it will return, maybe not.

Yet you could make notes of what you want to record as soon as you hear an idea, just as a thought occurs to you. So keep a lap-top, notebook or pad handy. Have an ideas document for each area of your life. Whether you are in a meeting or on your own, don't wait until the thought has been and gone.

As you listen to what is said, to your thoughts and reflections, sift for meaning. Don't go to a meeting, go away, then try to remember what was said. Write notes as the meeting progresses. Don't use up valuable post-meeting time writing a report that you could have written as you went along.

Years ago, in the pre-lap-top age, I used to attend a meeting for which I had volunteered to produce meeting notes. I wanted to make sure we caught the good ideas and were clear about who needed to do what. I would write up the notes and slip out the partially completed text towards the end of the meeting. When it finished, there were usually only a few points to add. The typed report was out five or ten minutes after the meeting finished. Others were impressed. These days, that kind of thing is easy to achieve. You can distribute the typed report by e-mail or via printer and paper copy in just a few minutes. This has the advantage that people can still remember what happened. It also tends to prompt quicker action.

Keep the notes in a notebook or your Day Book unless you tap them straight into a lap-top. Name and date your notebook and name and date each meeting. You don't have to write everything down. Decide what's important and worth recording as you listen. You will be able to retrieve your notes very quickly without having to write them up afterwards. Don't use loose leaf notes, since they can be too easily mislaid, and afterwards need to be filed.

Ideas need a context. One way to generate ideas is continually to ask yourself questions. How could we solve this problem? What would be a good way to cater for that? Wait for the answers to come. Your subconscious may do its best. Some people literally sit and wait for ideas.

Here's another way to get context. Over the next day or so, look at all the objects and services you use and note whether they are designed perfectly from your perspective. How would you improve them? Before long you will be coming up with much better ways to provide services. Your mind is like a muscle. The more you demand from it, the more it becomes capable of delivering.

Self Check

1. Do you make a note of good ideas?
2. Do you make meeting notes during the meeting?
3. Do you keep them in a Day Book?
4. Do you sometimes lose notes you have made?
5. Do you ask yourself good questions?
6. Do you wait for the answers?

5.8 Continually develop yourself

De-skilling doesn't save time, but re-skilling does

There is no limit to what you can achieve if you set about it with diligence and determination. In the short run, the biggest constraints upon your performance lie in your attitudes, skills and knowledge. In the long run, you can develop all of them so that they need not constrain you at all. I am not thinking of a one-off improvement. I am thinking of a continuing commitment to self-development, year in year out. What the Japanese call *Kaizen*.

Transforming yourself overnight is not realistic; doing so over the next five years is. You can develop your skills and habits every day. Incrementally. Bit by bit.

If you tried to build a new house in a day it would never stand, but if you allow yourself a few years you could have the house of your dreams. It's the same with your skills.

You are the person who can improve your own performance. You are responsible – or, as others say, 'response-able'. And you know that however good you already are, you can do better. As the saying goes: 'Good better best, let it never rest, 'til your good is better and your better's best.' I am not sure about the 'let it never rest' point, since we all need time to re–create.

You know that if you don't work to improve your own performance it may not improve at all. In fact it's likely to gradually worsen.

Fast changes in today's markets and technological tools mean there is a continuing imperative to get trained in what's coming up. You need to stay aware of how the world is changing. You could commit yourself to reading a skills-related book or an audio tape course each month. You would get through a dozen a year. Is that enough? My experience is that once you get into the habit of self-improvement you build a momentum which allows you to make further gear shifts.

Yesterday's skills will not do. If you don't learn tomorrow's ways, you will be lost. At the very least, an executive's relative performance and value will deteriorate fast without developing skills.

Imagine that one executive spends 5 per cent of the time developing new skills and another invests 15 per cent. Which of the two will be more effective in a year or two? Maybe even in a week or two? And will the executive who spends just 5 per cent of the work time on skills development ever catch up? Failing to invest a significant part of your time in developing yourself is myopic.

You may have a problem finding that extra 10 per cent of time to improve your performance. If that's really so, start with things you could learn that would provide an immediate payback in the time saved.

How could you best develop your skills? In which areas would you want to make a rapid improvement if you knew you could? Maybe your effectiveness could be improved in all sorts of humdrum ways. When did you last lose time because you couldn't find something? Fixing that might save you time fast. When did you last get held up because someone didn't co-operate with you, maybe even because someone doesn't appreciate you? Working on that relationship will take time: but failing to straighten it out may cost you time, over and over again. Or maybe you lost out because you just didn't know how to do something? De-skilling doesn't save time, but re-skilling does.

The habit of constant improvement needs to be built into your monthly routine. Maybe you should spend 10 per cent of your working time developing your skills. That's half a day a week. Could there be a better way to spend that time? Who would you rather invest in? Maybe you should be in touch with current developments in management thinking.

So what would you like to improve this week? You may not need a course. There are so many ways to gain skills, of which reading books like this is just one. With greater knowledge and skills, you are likely to come through the next crisis or crises more effectively and more confidently than you would otherwise, and with less pain.

Self Check

1. Whose responsibility is it to improve yourself?
2. How much knowledge do you need to gain each year to stand still?
3. How have your personal skills improved in the past year?
4. What are the main weaknesses you have identified recently in yourself?
5. What are you planning to do about any of them?
6. What efforts have you made to keep up with new technology?
7. How could you do your job more effectively?
8. What opportunities does new technology allow for improvement?
9. Which management thinkers have helped you recently?
10. Which books or audio tapes have assisted you?
11. How much of your time are you spending developing your skills?

5.9 Stay in good health

If good health is the result, what's the cause?

Your physical, mental and spiritual health are inter-related. If you are physically unwell, you won't be at the top of your form intellectually either.

It may be unusual to refer to health in the context of personal effectiveness, but it's difficult to be effective if you aren't well. Even those of us who aren't sick vary in the degree to which we are well. Few of us have the energy of athletes, even though being an executive can require vast amounts of it.

Who is responsible for your health? Your parents, your partner, your genes? None of them! *You* are responsible. You can affect your health massively. Doctors can sometimes help when you get sick, but you don't want to get to that point, if you can help it.

Have you noticed how your diet has an impact on your well-being, even your ability to think? What you eat affects the quality of your blood which in turn affects pretty much everything. The absence of exercise can also leave you feeling sluggish and reduce your powers of concentration. The less exercise you take, the less fit you will be.

Regular exercise and proper breathing can have a powerful effect. If you don't exercise, your muscles will atrophy. You should exercise several times a week, and do so sufficiently to raise the speed of your breathing and your heartbeat for at least twenty minutes.

You may feel you haven't enough time to better yourself in this way – but do you really need to watch another television series? Will that take you forward in any way? Suppose you cut all soaps out of your life, would you be any the worse for it? Think what you could do with all that time.

You might say you still don't have time to exercise. But once you have made the time, you will work better and more quickly which saves you time. So the net time cost of taking adequate exercise is zero or less!

You may take your breathing for granted, but how well do you breathe? Many people breathe too shallowly. They simply take oxygen into the top third of their lungs alone. Even when taking small routine breaths it's much better to fill the lower third of your lungs. To do so, push down on the diaphragm so that your tummy goes out as you breathe in. Try it.

If you don't breathe properly, you reduce your aerobic capacity. You have less energy. Work gets harder rather than easier.

You need to keep your mind in trim too. In some respects your work may do this, but there may be periods when your work isn't giving you enough of the right mental exercise. Your brainpower may diminish through lack of exercise; but, you can build it up.

You can feast your mind on inspiring literature. There are plenty of helpful management books and uplifting biographies. You don't need to think everything out for yourself from zero. You can drink from the wisdom of the ages and sip the wisdom of today.

135

Highly healthy people can achieve a lot more than those who aren't so well, and they can have a lot more fun along the way. They also tend to live longer.

Self Check

1. Who is responsible for your health?
2. Do you notice what you eat?
3. Does it seem to have an impact on your effectiveness?
4. Do you eat sufficient fruit and vegetables?
5. Do you take physical exercise several times a week?
6. Do you breathe properly?
7. How do you keep your mind in trim?

5.10 Avoid being ineffective

We see poorly through the mask of fear

Do you remember times when you were very successful and other moments when you were not? What were the main differences in your behaviour? Can you recall the tyranny of unfinished business? You may remember tasks you never completed, and then there's the work which you thought was OK, but someone else didn't, and he or she happened to be your boss. All of which begs the question, why are people ineffective? We take our eye off the ball, confuse ourselves and fail to use our judgement. We don't work out what we should do, or do it well.

Have you ever found yourself hanging around at your desk, nervously wondering what you should do and, finding no answer, continued to hang around? You don't want to be there, and you don't really need to be there, but it's in the nature of work that some projects go on hold. It's then that you need fillers, things that you can always do, any time. For instance, can't you get out one of the books you plan to read this month? Or can't you review your monthly goals and dwell on them for a while. If they are good goals, and as yet incomplete, something is likely to come up.

Rather than focus on the desired result *we* want, we sometimes try to second-guess others. We do what we think would impress them, and we often guess wrongly or look as though we are play acting. We think of what we would have to do to please them rather than what we should do. We rely on others to do our thinking even when we can be better informed. Losing sight of our objective is a major cause of ineffectiveness.

Sometimes we worry and act out of fear, causing things to go wrong. When we are scared, we usually aren't able to see what is actually happening. We see poorly through the mask of fear. How much clearer are faithful eyes!

Perhaps we want to appear to be something we are not, and we worry about being exposed; or something seems as though it is likely to go wrong and we think about the consequences of failure rather than how to succeed. We are in survival mode, nothing more, so our plans are scant and our actions uncoordinated. Being defensive, we focus on ourselves, so we are unable to see the situation, much less deal with it effectively. We complicate things horribly until no one can work them out, not even ourselves. Fear is a common cause of non-performance. O what a tangled web we weave, when first we practise to deceive!

Self Check

1. Do you sometimes lose sight of your objectives?
2. Do you sometimes allow fear to influence your actions?
3. How do things tend to go when you are fearful?
4. What steps could you take to deal with the fear?

5.11 Be different

What's you, about you?

The business world appears to be packed with people who are

trying to be the same as one another. They are following the crowd, but the crowd is going nowhere. You want to make your own way in the world. You want to have a point of difference, something that's a bit special. For one thing, it makes you easier to remember.

There are plenty of ways to be different and develop an edge at the same time, and the point of difference doesn't have to be directly connected with work. Your only problem is choosing one. For instance, you could learn an Asian language. How many people in your organization speak Chinese? More than a thousand million people do, but precious few Europeans. You could become an expert in something, however specialized – maybe a particular period in history or one foreign culture. A friend of mine developed some special areas of expertise and his general knowledge so that he nearly won *Mastermind* a few years ago. Or you could finally learn the piano and practise until you play it well. You could run a Youth Club, stand for your local council, or write a helpful book.

You can bring the experience of a different set of rules to bear in your work and develop your self-discipline at the same time. What's more, you will begin to stand out from the apparently grey men and women.

Self Check

1. What could you do well?
2. What would you like to discover?
3. What skills would you like to practise?
4. What's always interested you?
5. How could you make a unique contribution?
6. What's different about you?

5.12 Act with integrity

You can work with integrity or you can disintegrate

Think about the people you work with. Do they do what they

say? You probably have a pretty good idea of the likelihood that anyone will complete a particular task, and how well they will do it. We are all open books to one another if not to ourselves, so our integrity, or lack of it, is obvious in our actions, or lack of them.

Customers, suppliers and colleagues all have some freedom to determine how well they will work with a particular individual. They may not even think about it consciously, but they can give priority to one person's work over another based upon a number of factors. One of these is likely to be a person's integrity.

That doesn't mean that most people will refuse point blank to work with someone who lacks integrity, but they may not give it their best shot. And they may not want to get too close to that person.

Do you tell the truth about the work that needs to be done? Telling the truth is telling it as it is. It's crucial to success in business. If you find yourself dealing with someone who is dishonest, whether they are a client, supplier or colleague, you know they have crossed a line. They talk about things that don't exist, or at least don't exist the way they would have you believe. You know that what they say may be worthless and that it could be dangerous to rely on their word. You could show them how a trustworthy person acts, or create another option which doesn't involve working with them.

Do they specify clearly what is needed and when? Is your own role in the process clear? Have they even given these matters sufficient thought? How about your own performance on these matters?

You may think that business and ethics are strangers to one another and that a book about business ethics could be one of the shortest ever written. Some think business executives are greedy people who are out for themselves. They imagine that business executives will trample over others to get what they want, that business people think they are better than others, that business executives earn high salaries for doing little real work.

My experience is that business is as ethical as the people who are in it. It just poses some ethical challenges. Some business people may be greedier than some people who aren't involved in business – they tend to be directly involved with money and their greed may be more obvious to onlookers. Some business executives may think that they can get their success at the expense of others, that they may do well by doing others down. In some circumstances in life it's possible to do well for a while by taking from others, but there's normally a payback.

Trade is central to business life. One person renders a product or service and the other gives money. Each party chooses whether or not to make the trade. Each party trades only if it thinks it will be better off by doing so. You hire me or you don't hire me. I buy your product or I don't buy your product. You buy shares in my company or you don't buy shares in my company. We choose freely. Neither party forces the other to do anything.

In these circumstances, trampling over other people just won't work. For one thing, they are unlikely to agree to the trade. Even if they do agree because it is less bad than the alternative facing them, they are unlikely to trade with the would-be trampler again, and they are likely to pass on that message to others. An effective business person will always try to ensure that the other people involved feel that they have benefited from the arrangements.

The reason is simple. People like to do business with people whom they can trust. They don't like doing business with people who give them reasons not to trust them. It's much more hazardous. And, to some extent, almost everyone can choose with whom they do business.

The balance of forces in business isn't always equal. A client may feel he is in a much stronger position than a supplier, which may explain why some people seem to treat their clients well while treating their suppliers badly. This is usually an illusion. Most people who behave badly towards their suppliers behave equally badly towards their clients, they just do it behind their back. They may not know they are doing it but they talk to them nicely on the phone and then criticize them once the receiver is replaced. Effective executives have just one face and the people around them know it. They do what they say they will do.

People who deceive suppliers will sooner or later deceive

clients, and deceive colleagues too. So watch out for them. Try not to let them draw you in too far. If you are invited to join in a deceit, simply ask whether that would be telling the truth. Most people think themselves honest, and will shy away from an acknowledged lie.

You can't be dishonest in some parts of your business life and honest in the rest of your life. Your conscience won't manage it. You'll average out. Try and up your average.

Ethics is much more than telling the truth. It may mean far more than just doing what you think you should do. If you want to be successful in your home and family life, as well as your business and voluntary life, you need to be ethical. It means doing what colleagues, customers and other stakeholders can reasonably suppose you would do: act in their best interest as well as your own.

Would you like to work with people who are untrustworthy? If you don't want to work with such people, do you think other people do? Very few people really want to work with others who don't deserve their trust. We want to trust. We want to be trusted.

The successful executive's ethics are underpinned by values. They are the things we believe in. They come from inside us and are distinct from whims which come from outside us. Suppose you have committed yourself to completing a job today. Your values include doing the things you have promised you will do, but today's work has tired you and you want to rest. Your values say you should finish the work, your whim is to stop and relax. Which will win?

Self Check

1. Do you tell the truth about the work that needs to be done?
2. Would you want to be successful at other people's expense?
3. Do you behave well towards your colleagues, customers and suppliers?
4. Do you behave as well towards them as you want them to behave towards you?
5. When the chips are down, do the courtesies go out the window?
6. Do you try to do deals which really aren't in other people's interest too?
7. Do you try to sell people what they don't need?
8. Do you think through what their best interest might be?
9. If they knew how you really behave would they think any the worse of you?

Chapter Six

The Complete Canvas

Successful executives may not work more hours than the ineffective executive. You don't neglect important relationships outside work, any more than you neglect work itself. How could it be right to do so? Anyway, who really wishes to spend more time at the office? You may find yourself in a company where there is a culture of staying late, whether your work is done or not. Where people make supposedly witty comments like 'Thanks for popping in,' when you leave in good time. These people may need help, either because they have too much to do or because they are not getting their work done, or haven't achieved very much and want to compensate by being around.

6.1 Concentrate on the causes

Affect the cause, and you have the effect

Almost all executives spend most of their time dealing with the effects of others' actions. Now and again, they make time to think through the effects that they want to have. Generally speaking, the more time they make to do this, the more effective they will be. Even so, within an organization, you can't avoid spending some time dealing with effects. Mopping up is so very hard to do.

Problems are myriad. Nothing in executive life runs perfectly smoothly, nor will it. You'll notice things going better or worse than expected, things arriving early or late; you'll see the unanticipated causing problems left right and centre; and however often you mop up the mess, there's always another spillage waiting to happen. How should you respond?

Start by supposing that effects have causes. In other words, that organizational life isn't random. Consequently, something that goes wrong once will probably go wrong again – in all probability it has gone wrong before – unless some action is taken.

Once you have dealt with any pressing mess, you can accept a continuing repetition of each problem, or you can look for the cause. Most successful executives concentrate their energies on the cause of the problems. By dealing successfully with one cause, you may pre-empt a score or even a hundred similar problems. Think of all the time you may save, and all that stress.

For instance, take missed deadlines. You may come across them regularly. To the successful executive, they may suggest weak planning skills. Time being frittered away checking on the progress of jobs may suggest a low level of trust. Missed forecasts may suggest over-optimism. Unproductive meetings suggest insufficient preparation, and so on.

Once you are dealing with causes, you may find that all causes are of one particular type or another. So when you come across a 'cause', your first question may be: 'Is this cause of a type we have come across before?'

Now you are beginning to work at an even more powerful level, because you aren't addressing just one cause, you are beginning to address a common cause. Doing so successfully will take time. You can't cancel common causes quickly.

Some people may expect deep problems to be fixed in a day or two. They might imagine that issuing a memo saying 'Plan carefully', or 'Trust your suppliers' or 'Forecast realistically' or 'Prepare for meetings', will do it. It won't. You'll do well to deal with one such significant problem every quarter year, and you won't do it on your own. In the meantime, you can at least console yourself with the thought that you understand why something which may be profoundly irritating goes on occurring. And you know that the cause need not be there forever.

Self Check

1. What are the problems you regularly need to deal with?
2. What causes each of those things to happen?
3. What is similar about some or all of these causes?
4. What practical steps could you take to make a recurrence less likely?
5. How could you see things working better?
6. What behaviour would have to change?
7. What attitudes would need to change?
8. What new skills, if any, are required?
9. What new procedures, if any, would be likely to have an effect?

6.2 Visualize the vision

As you see, so it may be

The successful executive knows it doesn't have to be like this, however it is. Nothing is a given, unless you accept it as such.

A vision of how things could be enables the successful executive to spot quickly the difference between the way things are and the way they could be.

In the short run, the ideal may be unattainable, or simply too expensive, but you won't know how to attain it until you have envisaged it.

Top athletes use envisioning to see themselves performing well. Runners see themselves bursting through the tape. Few executives use the same technique, but seeing things going well repeatedly reprogrammes your subconscious and affects your behaviour powerfully, so that the events you envisage are much more likely to occur. See yourself being successful. See your organization being successful. See good relationships between the people within your organization and its associates.

This has an immediate benefit. In your mind, you are already experiencing some of the success. You believe that the difficulties of the present may be overcome. To that extent, they are less of a burden. You know they are temporary.

To the visualizer, the rest of mankind has its head in the sand. It is dealing with what is, while the visualizer sees what is yet to be.

Self Check

> 1. How well do things around you work?
> 2. How well could you visualize things working?
> 3. What else could you visualize?
> 4. What would things going well look like?

6.3 Go the extra mile

To enjoy more, deliver more

You can do any task extremely well, well, satisfactorily or poorly. You may never run out of opportunities to do things exceedingly well, but you may never have the opportunity to do this job well again.

You can shine at everything you do. The successful executive has the habit of doing things extremely well. Specifically, the successful executive renders more service than is required. The product stays the same, but the service makes all the difference.

It might take you no more time to complete work consistently a bit ahead of schedule, just better organization. Producing work to a higher standard might make your work significantly more effective, so saving time. Providing more than is asked for is likely to bring its own rewards.

Once you have received a task, set aside some time – it may be only a few minutes – to think about what is really wanted. While you are thinking about the best way to deliver, consider how you could provide more than has been asked for. How could you exceed the quality requirement? How could you simply deliver more? Would it take you an inordinate amount of time to do so? Could you deliver significantly sooner than requested? Can you deliver for much less than the budget? Quality, quantity, time and cost may be set for the average executive, but you don't have to be the average executive, you can be the successful executive.

You could find a different way of tackling the task or a different way of delivering the finished service. The means may not be stipulated in the brief. You can deliver with a smile.

Self Check

1. How could you provide more value in your day to day tasks?
2. How could you do your work better?
3. What extra touches might be appreciated?
4. How could you provide more than is asked for?
5. How could you exceed the quality requirement?
6. How could you simply deliver more?
7. Could you deliver significantly sooner than requested?
8. Can you deliver for much less than the budget?

6.4 Be effective outside work too

You can set as high standards outside work as in it

There's more to life than doing the job you are paid for – more even than doing it superbly well. There's a whole world outside your organization. You can make an impact there too. You may find great opportunities to prepare for future work through what you do in and around your current work, and through things that you do which have no obvious connection with your work.

There was a time when some organizations liked to own their executives. They wanted their executives' lives to be dominated by the firm, with very little else going on. These days, you may encounter a greater willingness to recognize that achievements outside work, whether in sports, community activities or elsewhere, add to the quality of the people who undertake them and so bring benefits for the firm. In any event, if a firm finds that its staff put most of their creative energy into other areas, it's up to the firm to allow people to take on bigger challenges at work.

Successful executives are effective at home too. (This doesn't mean that you treat your spouse the way you would treat another executive. This might be misunderstood!) Think about it. If you are ineffective at home, if the quality of your relationships isn't that good, isn't that likely to affect how you feel, and the way you relate to people at work – maybe making you a little bit less open, a little bit less understanding, a little bit less human?

Some people who seem to be quite effective at work are less so in other areas of their life. You can apply your business skills to personal chores too. Think about your flat or house. Are there any tasks outstanding? Tasks that may have been hanging over you for some time? Maybe your home isn't quite the way you would like it, but you don't have any plans to have it the way you want.

Take an area like your personal papers – things like birth and insurance certificates, bank statements and guarantees. If you don't organize them well, they are likely to trip you up, and in the meantime you have a nagging worry that there might be a problem. But it will take only a few hours to get a filing cabinet, set up the files the way you want them, and put your personal papers into them. If they are scattered about the place and you don't know quite where they are, you can put them into the files as you come across them. Once done, you won't have to worry about finding your passport the next time you have to go overseas!

Bills need not catch you out if you pay them on time! Keep a bills-to-pay file and review it regularly, or write the cheques as soon as you have opened the bill's envelope. Issue post-dated cheques if it's appropriate or set yourself up with a telephone banking facility. Write on the bill that you have paid it or chuck it in a bills-paid file or throw it out. Whatever.

Your family will need your attention too: mother, father, brother, sister, partner – children if you have them. What can you do to help each family member? How can you show them how to be more effective?

Do you have a problem remembering people's birthdays? Check them out at the beginning of the year and write them all in your diary. Make entries a week or so ahead if you want to be sure to send a card, letter or gift.

Your contribution need not be limited to your work, family and friends. You may get tremendous enjoyment from being active in a voluntary organization too. It gives you experience of a different environment which may enrich your life and may even help you to be more effective in your normal job. Working in one of them may support your personal mission. Voluntary organizations are different. This doesn't mean you drop all your business disciplines, but you may need to have plenty of patience. Many otherwise professional people approach them unprofessionally, but charities and other voluntary organizations need good executives.

In some ways, working with volunteers requires even greater executive skills to get to anything like the same level of effectiveness. Volunteers don't take orders, which may be one of the reasons why they volunteered. You have to be really understanding. You have to work within people's limitations, which can vary hugely. There's not much you can do if they don't want to get on with it. You need to coax them.

This is good practice for work. You may think that people do take any orders you give in your normal work. They may even look as though they are taking them. But if you haven't persuaded them, the effectiveness of your order will amount to next to nothing.

Self Check

1. How does your home life affect the way you feel?
2. How do your feelings affect the way you are at work?
3. How could you be more effective at home?
4. What important tasks are still to be done at home?
5. How can you help other members of your family to be more effective?
6. What skills do they need?
7. What business skills could you bring to a voluntary body?

6.5 The successful executive's manager

Everybody needs a good coach

The successful executive's manager enables executives to be successful. Successful managers are coaches, not stars. They may not appear to do very much themselves and may seem quite relaxed. They confirm the rules, show how the principles apply in any particular situation, show other people the way and then let them do things. They build up their team and try to increase the team's ability to perform. The members of their team come first, their own performance comes second.

Successful managers understand that their team can achieve anything, given good coaching. They constantly work to increase the team's capability and its actual performance. They set high standards and demand the best from people. They let you know that they expect you to do well and that they believe in you. The best managers will often have more faith in the team as a whole than the individual team members. The manager's belief should gradually convey itself to the team.

Successful managers aren't oblivious to people's weaknesses. They'll notice what people are good and bad at and try to ensure that they are in a position to do as much good work as possible. Successful managers play to people's strengths.

Unsuccessful managers may work flat out. They get in other people's way. They slow them down. They throw in their own solutions before an executive comes up with proposals. They change the job specification mid-way through. They don't respect others' space. They progress chase unnecessarily. They work for themselves not the team. The team is a means to the unsuccessful manager's personal ends.

Most executives are or will become managers. While you are an executive, you have a good opportunity to notice what does and doesn't make a good manager. Managers manage people and projects. They manage people to get them to complete projects on time and on budget. Their own performance becomes less important than the performance they can encourage from others. They need to show direction and pace and review progress from time to time.

A manager who helps a team to work 10 per cent more effectively will do better than a manager who helps himself to be 20 per cent more effective.

A successful manager never knows quite how much the team might achieve. That manager won't ever set a ceiling. Initially, the effective manager will review work closely to see what sort of standard each executive wants to set, and may not need to superimpose standards at all. The executive's own standards could match or even exceed those the manager would set, and a self-imposed standard usually has more force. The effective manager uses the team not only to do the work, but also to set standards wherever possible. What the effective manager doesn't do is to specify the method. The moment a manager specifies a method, the executive is freed of responsibility – and anyway, the executive may well come up with a better method.

There are three ways successful managers teach: by example, by example and by example. One manager I worked with had me in for a daily review meeting during a critical phase of a project I was running. I thought I knew my stuff. He made a note of every important thing we touched upon. Before long, I noticed that he could, and did, look back in his notebook to see what we said about something the day before, or even the week before. He wasn't telling me to take notes. That was for me to discover. He just showed me.

A good manager shows belief in the team. A new manager once needed to lay his hands on an important document and asked me for it. It wasn't my document or my responsibility, but he told me I had the best organizational and retrieval skills around. What do you suppose happened? Of course, I found it for him. He believed in me, so I believed in us. What's more, I was keen to get my next project from him.

Effective managers don't hang on to projects themselves. They delegate. They pass the ball. They get it out of the ruck as quickly as possible and give a good clean pass. Then they watch what happens.

They try to ensure that the overall task is expressed clearly. As far as possible, it is likely to be expressed in the form of a 'physical deliverable'. That may be a paper, a presentation, a delivery or the construction of a building.

If an overall project timetable has yet to be created, they'll ask for that before anything else, and try to guide the overall sequence of what needs to be created.

They don't crowd their own team. When they have regular review meetings with each executive, they may let the executive set the agenda. The manager is thus sending a signal that it is up to the executive to prepare for the meeting and take a view on what needs to be considered. The manager can quickly discover what the executive thinks is important, and how open he is being about any problems he is encountering and their solution.

As far as possible, the manager won't even suggest solutions that the executive might come up with himself. When a manager suggests solutions, the executive thinks he needn't bother — it must have been up to the manager all along; the delegation was just a routine; he was asking for a 'yes' man. Also, when the manager comes up with his own solution, he relieves the executive of the responsibility to make it work, so the implementation tends to get a bit weaker.

How much more powerful when the manager holds out until executives come up with a solution which the manager merely approves, and which the executives then implement knowing that it is their plan. After all, it's easy to implement someone else's plan, and if it doesn't work, too bad! Maybe it was a duff plan.

Once as a manager, I had executives regularly coming to me to ask what they should do about this, that or the other. Having some experience of the work, I could usually see a way of attempting to resolve the problem of the moment. Instead, I usually asked them questions like 'What's the problem?' 'What do you think you should do about it?' 'What would happen if you did that?' 'What else could you do?' and so on as necessary. This helped me to understand what was going on in my division, how they saw the situation, and any differences between the way they saw it and the way I saw it. As time went by, they came to me less and less. They realized they knew how to resolve the vast bulk of the difficulties to their own satisfaction.

Self Check

---

1. Are you, or would you be, an effective manager?
2. Would you be clear as to what team members might achieve?
3. Would you check that they understood their tasks?
4. Would you be willing to rely on them?
5. Would you trust them and let them know that you trust them?

6.6 The successful executive's director

The buck stops with the directors

Successful directors have helicopter vision. Hovering above day to day events, they can relate them to the overall picture they can see. They put events into context and provide leadership and a framework within which executives can be effective.

They don't step into the frame themselves. That would risk getting in the way of the executives. Within guidelines, they allow their teams to get on with the task in hand and the one after that.

Companies are legal entities, they are recognized in law as 'persons'. You can sue a company just like you can sue a person. Or you can sue the directors because they are deemed to be responsible for the affairs of the company you believe has wronged you. The directors are responsible in law for what happens at their company, even if they don't own it. They are responsible for that 'person', and they can be collectively responsible for anything done by any one director, or even something done by some of their staff. While shareholders have rights, directors have any number of obligations – at least in theory. In practice, directors may use company budgets to pay for professional advisers who can cover their every move so their risk is minimal.

Many executives become company directors, and most of the rest have to deal with directors sometime. Apart from having an elevated view of the firm, directors have a unique responsibility.

The directors are responsible to the company's shareholders. It's the shareholders' money that the company is using. Of course, companies may also borrow money from other sources. Typically, each board of directors reports to the shareholders in writing once a year. Directors and any interested shareholders attend the company's Annual General Meeting and that's where shareholders can quiz the directors on the annual report. Since each AGM will be likely to elect some of the board members, the shareholders could be powerful.

In practice, individual shareholders are powerless unless they own a majority of the company's shares, or can combine with other shareholders to get to a majority position. A 1 per cent vote for something has no impact. In the absence of bulk, disgruntled shareholders have just one remedy. They can sell their shares at the prevailing market price.

Company directors have to understand and keep up to speed with the financial aspects of their business. They really do need to read the papers which are typically circulated to directors a few days ahead of each board meeting. They also need to have a keen understanding of which are the key figures that really tell if the business is going forwards, backwards or sideways, and they should interest themselves in why it is going that way.

Directors should be independent. They should use their own experience and judgement to come to their own view on what is happening and why. They should be objective. They are trying to see what is really happening and match that against one or more of their past experiences.

What they mustn't do is simply believe what they are told by the operational staff, who have the strongest possible interest in putting things in a positive light. Mostly, staff hate coming forward with bad news. Directors should see the warning signs early and insist on appropriate action. Without getting too much in the way of day to day operation, they should have some separate communication channels with the rest of the company.

Directors are supposed to keep a company open if it should stay open and to close it if it needs to be closed. They recommend agreement to, or rejection of, any take-over bids by other companies. They are responsible for proposed acquisitions.

They need to scrutinize business plans. Especially those that require large borrowings or heavy expenditure. Will this investment really yield the projected revenue? What happens if the revenue is 15 per cent off? What if the cash flow is out by a month or two? How robust is the plan?

Company directors are often managing directors of their own division of the company. Managing directors are responsible for everything.

Directors are leaders or they are nothing. Every public action of theirs is a highly public action. It gets noticed. It gets remarked upon. It gets copied. Their absence can be noticed too. Directors can show the way. They can lead by example.

Self Check

1. Could you be an effective director?
2. What are the key factors that determine the success of your business?
3. As a director, what would you seek to change?
4. What standards would you set?

6.7 The successful executive's organization

The successful organization is a learning organization

The successful executive's organization will be one which empowers its executives. As they succeed, so the organization succeeds. Successful organizations help their customers and investors by providing value to them. Successful organizations have purpose, principles and procedures. Beyond that, it's down to the people. The purpose, principles and procedures will be in accord with one another, and understood by the people.

The successful organization won't do anything that isn't

done by the people within it. It will comprise a sufficient number of successful executives and it will encourage them to be effective. It will ensure that its executives understand exactly what being successful means, as well as the extent to which they are personally effective. This may mean telling executives when they have excelled, when they have done OK, or when performance needs to be improved. If the targets were clear enough and the guidelines were good enough, there might be nothing to tell. The result would already be known.

Goals will be set, but the successful organization knows that the best goals will be set by the executives themselves. They will be more likely to achieve them because those goals are more likely to be achievable and the executives will be more motivated. Some organizations already operate systems where the executives set their own business and personal goals for the year. Personal remuneration must depend to some extent upon the achievement of personal and company goals.

The same discipline applies to what the organization as a whole is about. What is it that its staff really want it to be about? What are its principles? How do its customers and suppliers see it? What do they think it can achieve?

The successful organization will support its executives. It will create the conditions in which they can excel. What sort of environments do your executives need? What kind of encouragements? In what kind of conditions do you do your best work?

It will strongly encourage executives to develop themselves. It will encourage them to assess themselves and identify the kinds of training and development upon which they should focus. The more they want to learn, the more they will do so.

The successful organization will provide value to customers, shareholders and employees – neglecting any one of these sectors could prove disastrous. It will also provide value to suppliers. I have seen organizations which treat their clients well while treating their suppliers badly. It doesn't work. If you don't have good relationships with your suppliers you won't maintain good relationships with your clients.

An effective organization will try to ensure that its suppliers feel at least as good about working with it, as they do about working with any other company. Moreover, it will actually want to help its suppliers to do good work and will try to encourage and maybe even train them because the more effective the supplier, the more effective its work will be for the organization. Also, the organization should be prized by the supplier as a client with good working practices. It will form a partnership between client and supplier. An organization will act like parents to its employees, a brother or sister to its customers and suppliers, and be the grown-up child of its shareholders.

The successful organization will get feedback on itself. Of course, it will measure the financial 'bottom line', but it will also look at more than its financial profit and its market share over time. The successful organization knows that these are both 'outcome measures' – they measure the outcome of other things which can themselves be measured – but also customers can tell you what they think of your product or service and, as often as not, how to improve it. Your suppliers can tell you about your operation, and the staff of your organization collectively understands it and individually can normally find lots of ways to improve it. If you discuss your plans with your shareholders, they may also be able to help.

Getting this feedback means listening. It means being relatively open in certain circumstances. It means having an organization where power does not depend upon the position of who had a good idea but on the power of the idea itself. It means a performance-based rather than a hierarchically based organization.

You might feel that your organization is imperfect; you may have spotted some weaknesses. You can respond to them in one of two ways. One is to criticize your own organization, but this won't help you to be productive or endear you to any managers who hear your criticisms out of context. The other way is first to think through what could be done to solve the problem that confronts you or others, and then find a good time to put your suggestion to someone who may listen to you. In other words, be constructive not destructive.

The successful organization doesn't bite off more than it can chew. It won't try to climb mountains in minutes. It makes sure it is properly prepared before it sets off on its next excursion. It maximizes the odds of success and minimizes the likelihood of failure, the likelihood of not completing the task because too many other things got in the way. It doesn't take on too much at once. It encourages a manageable amount of well-thought-through experimentation. An experiment which tells a company not to proceed any further is looked upon as a success as far as it goes.

Successful organizations don't merely try constantly to improve themselves. Nor do they simply settle for what works today. They try to re-invent themselves for tomorrow, before tomorrow arrives, and they try to do so at a measured pace: not too slow, not too quick.

Successful organizations are forever discovering the exceptional and turning it into the routine. They encode the exceptional, then they are able to keep on doing it. They like to find new and better things to do and new and better ways to do things. The discoveries then rapidly become the standard ways to work: wheels, once invented, are used throughout the organization. They encode the routine too, so you don't have to spend time thinking: How do I do this and how do I do that?' If 'this' or 'that' have been done before, the procedure becomes organizational knowledge.

In the information age, successful organizations are learning organizations, which are trying to develop their ability to learn from the present and develop into the future.

Self Check

1. What sort of environment do our executives need?
2. What kinds of encouragement should we give them?
3. Do they help to define their training requirements?
4. Do they set their own goals within an overall framework?
5. How can our organization improve itself?
6. How can it reinvent itself for tomorrow?
7. How can it incorporate the exceptional into its routines?

6.8 Stay well informed

In a time of change, you need to change yourself

You can apply robust skills and a healthy attitude inappropriately if you don't know what's going on around you. The less you study what's changing, the further you will get left behind. Watch the horizon. You need to keep retraining your sights.

This is an era of change. Whatever your work, organization and industry, it's changing rapidly, even if it's government (especially if it's government). The future will be different from the past, and predicting it is a hazardous pastime. Just staying in touch with the present takes time and effort. Nevertheless, you should constantly put even more time and effort into keeping up with what other people are doing. Colleagues and competitors can and will find better things to do and new ways to do things. Notice them and see how you could apply what they have discovered to your own work. You may be able to stretch their insight still further.

Perhaps your trade media will give you some information on what is changing. You may find that one or more national newspapers carry relevant features. What's happening in your company's New Product Development Department? What's working? What are your competitors up to? What new innovations are working well in other similar markets? How are other unrelated markets changing? What factors are driving the change? Might they drive change in your areas too?

One of the ways you will stay in touch is by asking people, 'What's new? What have you heard? What's changing? What do you see happening in future?' Listen carefully. Think as you hear. Use your eyes and ears. Use other people's eyes and ears too.

Self Check

1. What are your main sources of information?
2. What new things have you learnt in the past month?
3. Do you see the trade magazines?
4. What do they tell you about what is going on?
5. What's new? What's working?
6. What's been changing in your industry?
7. What do you think will change in future?

6.9 Tomorrow's executive

Tomorrow's executive can handle just about anything

'Let's forget about tomorrow', goes the song, 'because tomorrow never comes.' Well, it's here. And if you intend to go on being an executive for the next ten years or more you are going to be part of a quite different future. The challenges for executives are getting bigger and potentially more enjoyable too. For one thing, much of the drudgery is disappearing. A former colleague of mine retired in the 1980s after forty years service at the same firm. These days, lifetime employment has virtually disappeared. He told me that when he started working in accounts, you had to be strong simply in order to carry the ledgers (accounts books) around the building! Nowadays, there's more freedom, and with more freedom comes more responsibility. Within the parameters of corporate procedures, tomorrow's executives will make it up as they go along: 'Sort this, sort that, and sort how to do it.'

Automation has replaced the bulk of manual labour. Now computers are replacing most of routine management. With a doubling in computing power every eighteen months, computers will manage whatever is straightforward or even whatever is simply logical. Which means that executives won't be able to add much value simply by doing the routine. They'll have to think laterally.

Increasingly, executives won't be 'in accounts' since computers can do accounts. They won't be 'in operations' when that's mechanized too – they won't be anywhere in particular. Instead, executives will work in teams which will run projects.

As technology enables you to do more, you are expected to do more. Each change requires new working habits, which mean more learning. As the rate of change increases, your rate of learning must increase too. You'll have to find new ways to think. There's no more lugging ledgers to be done. And machines themselves are getting more friendly. Computers which can produce the spoken word in text format will eventually make typing as rare as the fountain pen.

Anyone who is already in business is likely to have to work especially hard to keep up with technology itself. To me, new software is awesome and each new thing I learn is a revelation. To children, it's just there. They accept it because it is what's around. They aren't fazed by it. They would no more get excited about its newness than I would get excited about TV. Wow, colour! Typically, the younger you are, the more easily you learn advanced computing, and the older you are, the more you have to work at it.

Tomorrow's executive won't think twice about getting needed files from the Internet or any associate's intranet. The successful executive will know how to search and where to look – and know all about what comes after the Internet too.

Organizations' loyalty to executives is diminishing. Jobs for life are being replaced by relatively short-term assignments which may be measured in a few years or even months. The stresses of expanding, contracting and expanding again make anything else impossible. Your company may not always be there when you want it to be there. It may not be able to stay with you through thick and thin, and it may not retrain you when the crunch comes.

You need to take the training that's offered when it is offered, and seek out more, both formal and informal. You will have more options when you are strong enough to leave the organization and stand on your own feet, or at least be attractive to a competitor. Not that I advocate going; always make the best of where you are. Your current organization could be right for you for the rest of your life. And even if it isn't, you could help to improve it.

Big organizations are shrinking as they contract out non-core activities. They are deciding to 'stick to the knitting'. Look at the contrast between Apple and Microsoft. Apple tried to provide software and hardware; Microsoft went for software only, and empowered others to make and market compatible hardware. Microsoft didn't necessarily have a better product, but it applied more power because it did less.

Firms are focusing on what they think they are really good at and trying to get even better at that one thing. Then they hire in specialist accountants, lawyers, marketers, property consultants, remuneration specialists, researchers and trainers, and whatever else they need, but only as and when they need them and for exactly as much as they need them. One huge company recently set up a big joint venture without a finance department. Instead, they are using an accountancy firm which, presumably, is good at that kind of thing. Think about it, companies without finance departments!

Organizations are becoming simply institutions which organize things. They may have few people on the payroll and even fewer physical assets, but they can get things done. An organization may really need ten specialists in one month, one in the next month and ten the month after. That's not a problem when the service is bought in. As firms specialize, they need generalists. This means that you need to be a generalist rather than a specialist if you don't want to get contracted out. The one thing you need to know in depth is the one thing that your firm does extremely well.

Make sure that your attitude, knowledge and skills would be sufficiently attractive to other companies or clients, should the music stop for you. It could stop any time.

Technology's ability to get all information to everybody means that most people need to become good at almost everything. It's still possible to be outstandingly good at one thing in particular, but the thing you will notice about most of the really successful executives is that they can handle just about anything. If they can't do it themselves, they know how to find someone who can. They are comfortable with words, numbers and people. They can get things done face to face or from continent to continent. They understand the dynamics of marketing, operations and finance. They can buy and sell.

They can start, manage and finish projects. How well does this describe you?

Remote working and home working makes it difficult for companies to measure the time that staff put into their work, so they have to measure what they produce instead. In turn, this helps liberate individuals to do their own work in their own time in the way that best suits them. If you can produce the same result with less effort in less time, you gain time for yourself. You probably gain more time for the firm as well.

Executive pay will change too since many executives won't be paid for their time. It won't matter to the firm whether they 'spend' more or less time on the task (as long as they get it done on schedule) since the firm won't pay them more if they spend more time. If anything, it should pay them more if they take less time since the output can be available quicker. Executives will be paid for the value they provide. And this will come about as it becomes so much easier to measure results. Precisely.

In fact, many of tomorrow's executives will be self-employed consultants. The firm will be able to use each 'executive' as much or as little as it likes, or it may commit a minimum amount of work, time or income. Such executives won't have 'dead time' at work. If they have nothing to do, they can take time out, or think about their next project in more pleasant surroundings. Organizations can stop using the self-employed executive anytime, but if the work is good, the firm may go on using the executive for as long as it goes on employing most of its remaining employees.

Most executives are still paid to turn up at their place of work. They have to 'go to work'. Tomorrow's executives won't be paid to hang around in an office – in fact they probably won't have an office, except the portable electronic one they plug in when they visit.

Self Check

1. Are you constantly developing your skills?
2. If your company had a free choice, would it want to hire you again?
3. Would a competitor want to hire you?
4. How risky is it if you are not sufficiently tooled up?
5. What skills are they looking for now?
6. What skills do you think they are likely to look for in the future?

6.10 Success for you and me

One person's success can also be another person's success

You can choose to be successful. You can also choose what success means for you. You don't have to accept your parents' definition of success, although it may be a good one, or your peers' definition, or even the world's definition of success. You can discover your own.

Others may have in mind what you should do, and they may be right or wrong. Unless you know what is right for you, you can't direct your life. There's no point rebelling against what anyone else might have in mind, until you have something with which to fill the void that would follow a successful rebellion. You don't need to fight against the world; you can discover its grain, and go with it.

We are all imbued, to varying extents, with the idea that someone's gain is another person's loss. It need not be so. Your success need not be someone else's failure. You can create something new which adds without taking away. Mostly, business is an exercise in extended co-operation, while competition is secondary. Incidentally, the root of the word competition means 'to petition together', so even competition itself is really about co-operation. We can petition the marketplace together!

Money is a mid-point on the path to success. For some, it's a mark of success because it's a measure of value. If you've earned a million, others should have received more than a million in value from you, otherwise they wouldn't have given you the money.

While you can do lots of things with money, it's not much good in itself. Just bits of paper or figures on a statement. It may provide a temporary sense of security, but money should never determine how you feel. Some years ago, I remember being anxious about my financial affairs and thinking I would feel better if I just had a few thousand pounds in a savings account. When I realized that I did indeed have that, the feeling of anxiety still remained. The money or lack of it wasn't making me anxious. I was.

You may feel money gives you room for manoeuvre, but there may be other ways to get that same room. Money may be useful as an indicator, yet you may find better, or more precise, measures of success.

However good you become at doing things, you may not long escape the question: what is it that you should be doing? You might sense that success has to do with fulfilling your mission – the purpose of your life. You might feel that you can make up your own mission or you might sense that it's just there waiting for you to uncover it. Why not suppose it exists and you are simply hunting for it? It may be so, and it would be a great shame to miss it.

Self Check

1. What's your definition of success?
2. How will you discover it?
3. What do you want to do about it?
4. What would be a successful life for you?

6.11 Changes

If it ain't broke, try to improve it

In economic terms, we change or we die. We become obsolescent if the market moves past us and on to pastures new. It's the same with organizations. Yesterday's winners become today's losers, unless they change.

Change involves costs. You need to invest time, and some-times money, to make change, so it's even harder to make

165

changes when you are losing. At that time, the temptation to get every hand to the pump and try to put out the fire is often irresistible. But you don't make the time to deal with what caused the fire in the first place. The best and least painful time to make change, to your organization or to yourself, is when things are going reasonably well.

It's so tempting to remain unchanged. Change means a violation of a system, habit, even of ourselves. That's why we need to make change a built-in part of our routine. Unavoidable. We should reverse the maxim, 'If it ain't broke, why fix it?' and instead say, 'If it ain't broke, try to improve it.'

6.12 What should you do now?

Preach what you practise

Put something into practice and notice your behaviour change. See how well you do. Don't be discouraged when you don't get it quite right. You can always make a mistake. The only question is, will you make the same mistake again, or will you take action to avoid a repetition? You may find your progress tends to be two steps forward, one step back, another two steps forward, and so on. There's no need to stay where you are.

You may have heard the story of the man who once gave a powerful sermon which engaged his audience. They returned next week and heard him give exactly the same sermon. The next week he gave it a third time. A group of elders of his Church congregated together to ask him, 'Are you aware that some of the words you are using are the same as you used last week?'

'You noticed,' he said, 'and I am going to go on giving the same sermon until you start living it.' Doing something once is rarely enough. Another man walked into a room and said to a woman, 'I tried those success tips you mentioned yesterday. What shall I do today?' The answer, of course, was to do more of the same.

Self Check

1. What could you put into practice today?
2. What could you put into practice this week?
3. What could you put into practice this year?

Index

167